STALIN

The Enduring Legacy

Kerry Bolton

STALIN

The Enduring Legacy

Kerry Bolton

Copyright © 2017 Black House Publishing Ltd

ISBN-13: 978-1-910881-62-0

Black House Publishing Ltd
Kemp House
152 City Road
London
UNITED KINGDOM
EC1V 2NX

www.blackhousepublishing.com
Email: info@blackhousepublishing.com

Contents

Foreword

Dr. Bolton's book on Stalinist Communism is a major contribution to the proper understanding of Russian, as well as American, politics and society in the twentieth century. It brushes aside the anti-Stalinist biases of the Trotskyist American chroniclers of this historical period to reveal the unquestionable integrity of Stalin as a nationalist leader. At the same time, it highlights the vital differences between the Russian national character rooted in the soil and history of Russia, and its opposite, the rootless Jewish cosmopolitanism that Trotskyist Marxism sought to impose on the Russians – as well as on the rest of the world. The struggle between folkish nationalist and international financial forces within Communism, however, was conducted through a long series of political power-struggles between the Stalinist and Trotskyist camps, in Russia as well as in America, and Bolton recounts these intrigues with riveting attention to detail. Indeed, the earlier, political section of the work has much of the gripping quality of a Le Carré novel - except that the reality on which Le Carré's novels were based is not only stranger than fiction but also more frightening.

Ironically, it is the last section of the book - on the western legacy of Stalinism among right-wing leaders who placed, and still place, their hopes on Russia as a potential power-base from which to counter the globalist agendas of the Trotskyists - that is the most disturbing, since it is plain to the reader here that the post-war resistance against the Titanic forces of Marx and Trotsky is not only disadvantaged in America by its separation from the native European soil and culture but also uncertain, in Europe, of finding a leader equal in stature to Stalin.

Alexander Jacob, Brno, September 2012

Introduction

Joseph Stalin's legacy continues to haunt geopolitical developments across the world. Stalin ('Man of Steel') ruled the USSR and later Soviet-Russian Empire with an iron fist from 1928 until his death in 1953. His individual resolve placed Russia on a course to national greatness by reversing the Bolshevik-Marxist psychosis that would have reduced Russia to chaos and destroyed the very soul of the Russian people.

In foreign policy Stalin assured Russia's place as a world power and maintained the national and cultural freedom of Russia by rejecting the post-1945 international policy that the USA aimed at creating a one-world government.

In the arts Stalinism repudiated 'rootless cosmopolitanism' in favour of a Soviet culture based on a synthesis of Russian traditions.

This writer contends that had it not been for Stalin, we would have been living under a one-world state decades ago, and existing as economic automatons at the behest of global capitalism. The contention is also that the USA has long been the centre of 'world revolution', and continues to be so, while Stalin pursued a most un-Marxist policy of nationalism and imperialism.

Stalinism therefore constitutes a major force for tradition and conservatism in the world, against globalisation; while the USA maintains its mission as a centre of contagion that spreads throughout the world.

Such views on the USSR and Stalin are not new. In the early days of the Stalinist regime many on the German Right believed that the Soviet Union would transcend Marxism and become a nationalist state, which might form an alliance with Germany against the plutocratic powers. This was a primary position of the German National-Bolsheviks, a faction of the Right. Even the conservative historian Oswald Spengler saw the same possibility. From the Soviet side, Russian diplomats in Berlin were instructed to cultivate ties with pro-Soviet elements in the Right-wing intelligentsia. After World War II, when the USA had fallen out with its Russian wartime ally and sought German assistance against the USSR in the Cold War, German Rightist war veterans, who had fought against Russia, refused to do so again under American direction. Major-General Otto Remer and the allegedly 'neo-Nazi' Socialist Reich Party regarded the USA as more dangerous to the soul and freedom of Germany and Europe than the USSR. In the USA a faction of the Right also regarded the USSR as having transcended Marxism in favour of cultural and political health, recognising that their own country was the real centre of international subversion and revolution.

This book examines how the legacy of Stalin has had a lasting impact upon the world, and why the course Russia took under Stalin continues to be relevant to the present and the future. It is not intended as an apologia for Stalin's crimes, for the Katyn massacre or the Ukrainian famine, etc. The bandying about of moralistic clichés about 'crimes against humanity' is often nothing but strategies to demonise one's political adversaries by those who are hardly innocent themselves. It is intended rather to realistically assess Stalin's impact on the present and coming struggles for world power, based on the belief that Russia must and will play a pivotal role in the shaping of a new geopolitical and cultural bloc that again says 'nyet' to the 'rootless cosmopolitans'.

I

Stalin's Fight Against International Communism

The notion that Stalin 'fought communism' at a glance seems bizarre. However, the contention is neither unique nor new. Early last century the seminal German conservative philosopher-historian Oswald Spengler stated that Communism in Russia would metamorphose into something distinctly Russian which would be quite different from the alien Marxist dogma that had been imposed upon it from outside. Spengler saw Russia as both a danger to Western Civilisation as the leader of a 'coloured world-revolution', and conversely as a potential ally of a revived Germany against the plutocracies. Spengler stated of Russia's potential rejection of Marxism as an alien imposition from the decaying West that:

> Race, language, popular customs, religion, in their present form… all or any of them can and will be fundamentally transformed. What we see today then is simply the new kind of life which a vast land has conceived and will presently bring forth. It is not definable in words, nor is its bearer aware of it. Those who attempt to define, establish, lay down a program, are confusing life with a phrase, as does the ruling Bolshevism, which is not sufficiently conscious of its own West-European, Rationalistic and cosmopolitan origin.[1]

Even as he wrote, Bolshevism in the USSR was being fundamentally transformed in the ways Spengler foresaw. The 'rationalistic' and 'cosmopolitan' origins of Bolshevism were soon being openly repudiated and a new course was defined by Zhdanov and other Soviet eminences.

---

1   Oswald Spengler, *The Hour of Decision* (New York: Alfred A Knopf, 1963), 61.

5

Contemporary with Spengler in Weimer Germany, there arose among the 'Right' the 'National Bolshevik' faction one of whose primary demands was that Germany align with the Soviet Union against the Western plutocracies. From the Soviet side, possibilities of an alliance with the 'Right' were far from discounted and high level Soviet sources cultivated contacts with the pro-Russian factions of the German Right including the National Bolsheviks.[2]

German-Soviet friendship societies included many conservatives. In Arbeitsgemeinschaft zum Studium der Sowjetrussichen Planwirtschaft (Arplan)[3] Conservative-Revolutionaries and National Bolsheviks comprised a third of the membership. Bund Geistige Berufe (BGB)[4] was founded in 1931 and was of particular interest to Soviet Russia, according to Soviet documents, which aimed 'to attract into the orbit of our influence a range of highly placed intellectuals of rightist orientation'.[5]

The profound changes caused Konstantin Rodzaevsky, leader of the Russian Fascist Union among the White Russian émigrés at Harbin, to soberly reassess the USSR and in 1945 he wrote to Stalin:

> Not all at once, but step by step we came to this conclusion. We decided that: Stalinism is exactly what we mistakenly called 'Russian Fascism'. It is our Russian Fascism cleansed of extremes, illusions, and errors.[6]

In the aftermath of World War II many German war veterans, despite the devastating conflagration between Germany and the USSR, and the rampage of the Red Army across Germany with Allied contrivance, were vociferous opponents of any German alliance with the USA against the USSR. Major General Otto

---

2   K R Bolton, 'Jünger and National-Bolshevism' in *Jünger: Thoughts & Perspectives* Vol. XI (London: Black Front Press, 2012).
3   Association for the Study of the Planned Economy of Soviet Russia.
4   League of Professional Intellectuals.
5   K R Bolton, 'Jünger and National-Bolshevism', op. cit.
6   Cited by John J Stephan, *The Russian Fascists* (London: Hamish Hamilton, 1978), 338.

E Remer and the Socialist Reich Party were in the forefront of advocating a 'neutralist' line for Germany during the 'Cold War', while one of their political advisers, the American Spenglerian philosopher Francis Parker Yockey, saw Russian occupation as less culturally debilitating than the 'spiritual syphilis' of Hollywood and New York, and recommended the collaboration of European rightists and neo-Fascists with the USSR against the USA.[7] Others of the American Right, such as the Yockeyan and Spenglerian influenced newspaper *Common Sense*, saw the USSR from the time of Stalin as the primary power in confronting Marxism, and they regarded New York as the real 'capitol' of Marxism.

What might be regarded by many as an 'eccentric' element from the Right were not alone in seeing that the USSR had undergone a revolutionary transformation. Many of the Left regarded Stalin's Russia as a travesty of Marxism. The most well-known and vehement was of course Leon Trotsky who condemned Stalin for having 'betrayed the revolution' and for reversing doctrinaire Marxism. On the other hand, the USA for decades supported Marxists, and especially Trotskyites, in trying to subvert the USSR during the Cold War. The USA, as the columnists at *Common Sense* continually insisted, was promoting Marxism, while Stalin was fighting it. This dichotomy between Russian National Bolshevism and US sponsored international Marxism was to having lasting consequences for the post-war world up to the present.

Stalin Purges Marxism

The Moscow Trials purging Trotskyites and other veteran Bolsheviks were merely the most obvious manifestations of Stalin's struggle against alien Marxism. While much has been written condemning the trials as a modern day version of the Salem witch trials, and while the Soviet methods were often less

---

7   K R Bolton, 'Francis Parker Yockey: Stalin's Fascist Advocate', *International Journal of Russian Studies,* Issue No. 6, 2010,
      http://www.radtr.net/dergi/sayi6/bolton6.htm

than judicious the basic allegations against the Trotskyites et al were justified. The trials moreover, were open to the public, including western press, diplomats and jurists. There can be no serious doubt that Trotskyites in alliance with other old Bolsheviks such as Zinoviev and Kameneff were complicit in attempting to overthrow the Soviet state under Stalin. That was after all, the raison d'etre of Trotsky et al, and Trotsky's hubris could not conceal his aims.[8]

The purging of these anti-Stalinist co-conspirators was only a part of the Stalinist fight against the Old Bolsheviks. Stalin's relations with Lenin had not been cordial, Lenin accusing him of acting like a 'Great Russian chauvinist'.[9] Indeed, the 'Great Russians' were heralded as the well-spring of Stalin's Russia, and were elevated to master-race like status during and after the 'Great Patriotic War' against Germany. Lenin, near death, regarded Stalin's demeanour as 'offensive', and as not showing automatic obedience. Lenin wished for Stalin to be removed as Bolshevik Party General Secretary.[10]

Dissolving the Comintern

The most symbolic acts of Stalin against International Communism were the elimination of the Association of Old Bolsheviks, and the destruction of the Communist International (Comintern). The Comintern, or Third International, was to be the basis of the world revolution, having been founded in 1919 in Moscow with 52 delegates from 25 countries.[11] Zinoviev headed the Comintern's Executive Committee.[12] He was replaced by Bukharin in 1926.[13] Both Zinonviev and Bukharin were among the many 'Old Bolsheviks' eliminated by Stalin.

Stalin regarded the Comintern with animosity. It seemed to

8   See Chapter III: 'The Moscow Trials in Historical Context'.
9   R Service, *Comrades: Communism: A World History* (London: Pan MacMillan, 2008), 97.
10   *Ibid.,* 98.
11   *Ibid.,* 107.
12   *Ibid.,* 109.
13   *Ibid.,* 116.

function more as an enemy agency than as a tool of Stalin, or at least that is how Stalin perceived the organisation. Robert Service states that Dimitrov, the head of the Comintern at the time of its dissolution, was accustomed to Stalin's accusations against it. In 1937 Stalin had barked at him that 'all of you in Comintern are hand in glove with the enemy'.[14] Dimitrov must have wondered how long he had to live.[15]

Instead of the Communist parties serving as agents of the world revolution, in typically Marxist manner, and the purpose for founding the Comintern, the Communist parties outside Russia were expected to be nationally oriented. In 1941 Stalin stated of this:

> The International was created in Marx's time in the expectation of an approaching international revolution. Comintern was created in Lenin's time at an analogous moment. Today, national tasks emerge for each country as a supreme priority. Do not hold on tight to what was yesterday.[16]

This was a flagrant repudiation of Marxist orthodoxy, and places Stalinism within the context of National Bolshevism.

The German offensive postponed Stalin's plans for the elimination of the Comintern, and those operatives who had survived the 'Great Purge' were ordered to Ufa, South of the Urals. Dimitrov was sent to Kuibyshev on the Volga. After the Battle of Stalingrad, Stalin returned to the issue of the Comintern, and told Dimitrov on 8 May 1943 to wind up the organisation. Dimitrov was transferred to the International Department of the Bolshevik Party Central Committee.[17] Robert Service suggests that this could have allayed fears among the Allies that Stalin would pursue world revolution in the post-war world. However,

---

14   G Dimitrov, Dimitrov and Stalin 1934-1943: Letters from the Soviet Archives, 32, cited by R Service, *Ibid.,* 220.
15   R Service, *Ibid.,* 220.
16   G Dimitrov, op. cit., cited by Service, *Ibid.,* 221.
17   R Service, *Ibid.,* 222.

Stalin's suspicion of the Comintern and the liquidation of many of its important operatives indicate fundamental belligerence between the two. In place of proletarian international solidarity, Stalin established an All-Slavic Committee[18] to promote Slavic folkish solidarity, although the inclusion of the Magyars[19] was problematic.

Stalin throughout his reign undertook a vigorous elimination of World Communist leaders. Stalin decimated communist refugees from fascism living in the USSR. While only 5 members of the Politburo of the German Communist Party had been killed under Hitler, in the USSR 7 were liquidated, and 41 out of 68 party leaders. The entire Central Committee of the Polish Communist Party in exile were liquidated, and an estimated 5000 party members were killed. The Polish Communist Party was formally dissolved in 1938. 700 Comintern headquarters staff were purged.[20]

Among the foreign Communist luminaries who were liquidated was Bela Kun, whose psychotic Communist regime in Hungary in 1919 lasted 133 days. Kun fled to the Soviet Union where he oversaw the killing of 50,000 soldiers and civilians attached to the White Army under Wrangel, who had surrendered after being promised amnesty. Kun was a member of the Executive Committee of the Comintern. A favourite of Lenin's, this bloody lunatic served as a Comintern agent in Germany, Austria and Czechoslovakia during the 1920s. In 1938 he was brought before a tribunal and after a brief trial was executed the same day.[21]

Another action of great symbolism was Stalin's moves against the 'Old Bolsheviks', the veterans of the 1917 Revolution. Leon Sedov, Leon Trotsky's son, in his pamphlet on the Great Purge

---

18 *Ibid.*
19 Hungarians.
20 Richard Overy, *The Dictators: Hitler's Germany and Stalin's Russia* (London: Allen Lane, 2004), 201.
21 L I Shvetsova, et al. (eds.), Rasstrel'nye spiski: Moskva, 1937-1941: ... Kniga pamiati zhertv politicheskii repressii. ('The Execution List: Moscow, 1937-1941: ... Book of Remembrances of the victims of Political Repression'), (Moscow: Memorial Society, Zven'ia Publishing House, 2000), 229.

of the late 1930s, waxed indignant that Stalin 'coldly orders the shooting of Bolsheviks, former leaders of the Party and the Comintern, and heroes of the Civil War'.[22] 'The Association of Old Bolsheviks and that of the former political prisoners has been dissolved. They were too strong a reminder of the "cursed" revolutionary past'.[23]

In place of the Comintern the Cominform was established in 1947, for the purpose of instructing Communist parties to campaign against the Marshall Aid programme that was designed to bring war-ravished Europe under US hegemony. 'European communism was to be redirected' towards maintaining the gains of the Red Army during World War II. 'Communist parties in Western Europe could stir up trouble', against the USA. The Cominform was far removed from being a resurrection of the old Comintern. As to who was invited to the inaugural meeting held at a secluded village in Poland, 'Stalin... refused a request from Mao Zedong, who obviously thought that the plan was to re-establish the Communist International'. The Spanish and Portuguese parties were not invited, nor were the British, or the Greek Communist Party, which was fighting a civil war against the royalists.[24]

The extent of the 'fraternity' between the USSR and the foreign Communists can be gauged from the delegates having not been given prior knowledge of the agenda, and being 'treated like detainees on arrival'. While Soviet delegates Malenkov and Zhdanov kept in regular communication with Stalin, none of the other delegates were permitted communication with the outside world.[25]

Repudiation of Marxist Doctrine

The implementation of Marxism as a policy upon which to construct a State was of course worthless, and Stalin reversed the doctrinaire Marxism that he had inherited from the Lenin regime. Leon Sedov indignantly stated of this:

---

22   L Sedov, 'Why did Stalin Need this Trial?', The Red Book on the Moscow Trials, http://www.marxists.org/history/etol/writers/sedov/works/red/ch01.htm

23   *Ibid.*, 'Domestic Political Reasons'.

24   R Service, op. cit., 240-241.

25   *Ibid.*, 242.

In the most diverse areas, the heritage of the October revolution is being liquidated. Revolutionary internationalism gives way to the cult of the fatherland in the strictest sense. And the fatherland means, above all, the authorities. Ranks, decorations and titles have been reintroduced. The officer caste headed by the marshals has been reestablished. The old communist workers are pushed into the background; the working class is divided into different layers; the bureaucracy bases itself on the 'non-party Bolshevik', the Stakhanovist, that is, the workers' aristocracy, on the foreman and, above all, on the specialist and the administrator. The old petit-bourgeois family is being reestablished and idealized in the most middle-class way; despite the general protestations, abortions are prohibited, which, given the difficult material conditions and the primitive state of culture and hygiene, means the enslavement of women, that is, the return to pre-October times. The decree of the October revolution concerning new schools has been annulled. School has been reformed on the model of tsarist Russia: uniforms have been reintroduced for the students, not only to shackle their independence, but also to facilitate their surveillance outside of school. Students are evaluated according to their marks for behaviour, and these favour the docile, servile student, not the lively and independent schoolboy. The fundamental virtue of youth today is the 'respect for one's elders', along with the 'respect for the uniform'. A whole institute of inspectors has been created to look after the behaviour and morality of the youth.[26]

This is what Leon Sedov, and his father, Leon Trotsky, called the 'Bonapartist character of Stalinism'.[27] And that is precisely what Stalin represents in history: the Napoleon of the Bolshevik Revolution who reversed the Marxian doctrinal excrescences in a manner analogous to that of Napoleon's reversal of Jacobin fanaticism after the 1789 French Revolution. Underneath the

---

26   *Ibid.*
27   *Ibid.*

hypocritical moral outrage about Stalinist 'repression', etc.,[28] a number of salient factors emerge regarding Stalin's repudiation of Marxist-Leninist dogma:

- The 'fatherland' or what was called again especially during World War II, 'Holy Mother Russia', replaced international class war and world revolution.

- Hierarchy in the military and elsewhere was re-established openly rather than under a hypocritical façade of soviet democracy and equality.

- A new technocratic elite was established, analogous to the principles of German 'National Bolshevism'.

- The traditional family, the destruction of which is one of the primary aims of Marxism generally[29] and Trotskyism specifically,[30] was re-established.

- Abortion, the liberalisation of which was heralded as a great achievement in woman's emancipation in the early days of Bolshevik Russia, was reversed.

- A Czarist type discipline was reintroduced to the schools; Leon Sedov condemned this as shackling the free spirit of youth, as if there were any such freedom under the Leninist regime.

- 'Respect for elders' was re-established, again anathema to the Marxists who seek the destruction of family life through the alienation of children from parents.[31]

---

28   Given that when Trotsky was empowered under Lenin he established or condoned the methods of jurisprudence, concentration camps, forced labour, and the 'Red Terror', that were later to be placed entirely at the feet of Stalin.

29   Karl Marx, 'Proletarians and Communists', *The Communist Manifesto*, (Moscow: Progress Publishers, 1975), 68.

30   K R Bolton, 'The State versus Parental Authority', *Journal of Social, Political & Economic Studies*, Vol. 36, No. 2, Summer 2011, 197-217.

31   K Marx, *Communist Manifesto*, op. cit.

What the Trotskyites and other Marxists objected to was Stalin's establishment of the USSR as a powerful 'nation-state', and later as an imperial power, rather than as a citadel for world revolution. However, the Trotskyites, more than any other Marxist faction, allied themselves to American imperialism in their hatred of Stalinist Russia, and served as the most enthusiastic partisans of the Cold War.[32] Sedov continued:

> Stalin not only bloodily breaks with Bolshevism, with all its traditions and its past, he is also trying to drag Bolshevism and the October revolution through the mud. And he is doing it in the interests of world and domestic reaction. The corpses of Zinoviev and Kamenev must show to the world bourgeoisie that Stalin has broken with the revolution, and must testify to his loyalty and ability to lead a nation-state. The corpses of the old Bolsheviks must prove to the world bourgeoisie that Stalin has in reality radically changed his politics, that the men who entered history as the leaders of revolutionary Bolshevism, the enemies of the bourgeoisie, - are his enemies also. Trotsky, whose name is inseparably linked with that of Lenin as the leader of the October revolution, Trotsky, the founder and leader of the Red Army; Zinoviev and Kamenev, the closest disciples of Lenin, one, president of the Comintern, the other, Lenin's deputy and member of the Politburo; Smirnov, one of the oldest Bolsheviks, conqueror of Kolchak—today they are being shot and the bourgeoisie of the world must see in this the symbol of a new period. This is the end of the revolution, says Stalin. The world bourgeoisie can and must reckon with Stalin as a serious ally, as the head of a nation-state…. Stalin has abandoned long ago the course toward world revolution.[33]

As history shows, it was not Stalin to whom the 'world bourgeoisie' or more aptly, the world plutocracy, looked on as an ally, but leading Trotskyites whose hatred of Stalin and the USSR made them vociferous advocates of American foreign policy.

---

32   See Chapter V.
33   L Sedov, op. cit., 'Reasons of Foreign Policy'.

Family Life Restored

Leon Trotsky is particularly interesting in regard to what he saw as the 'revolution betrayed' in his condemnation of Stalinist policies on 'youth, family, and culture'. Using the term *'Thermidor'*, taken from the French revolutionary era, in his description of Stalinism vis-à-vis the Bolshevik revolution, Trotsky began his critique on family, generational and gender relations. Chapter 7 of *The Revolution Betrayed* is worth reading in its entirety as an over-view of how Stalin reversed Marxism-Leninism. Whether that is 'good' or 'bad' is, of course, left to the subjectivity of the reader.[34]

The primary raison d'etre of Marxism for Trotsky personally seems to have been the destruction of religion and of family (as it was for Marx).[35] Hence, the amount of attention Trotsky gives to lamenting the return to traditional family relations under Stalin:

The revolution made a heroic effort to destroy the so-called 'family hearth' – that archaic, stuffy and stagnant institution in which the woman of the toiling classes performs galley labor from childhood to death. The place of the family as a shut-in petty enterprise was to be occupied, according to the plans, by a finished system of social care and accommodation: maternity houses, creches, kindergartens, schools, social dining rooms, social laundries, first-aid stations, hospitals, sanatoria, athletic organizations, moving-picture theaters, etc. The complete absorption of the housekeeping functions of the family by institutions of the socialist society, uniting all generations in solidarity and mutual aid, was to bring to woman, and thereby to the loving couple, a real liberation from the thousand-year-old fetters. Up to now this problem of problems has not been solved. The forty million Soviet families remain in their overwhelming majority nests of medievalism, female slavery and hysteria, daily humiliation of children, feminine and childish superstition. We must permit ourselves no illusions

---

34   L Trotsky, The Revolution Betrayed, Chapter 7, 'Family, Youth and Culture', http://www.marxists.org/archive/trotsky/1936/revbet/ch07.htm

35   K R Bolton, 'The Psychopathology of the Left', Ab Aeterno, No. 10, Jan,-March 2012, Academy of Social and Political Research (Athens), Paraparaumu, New Zealand. The discussion on Marx and on Trotsky show their pathological hatred of family.

on this account. For that very reason, the consecutive changes in the approach to the problem of the family in the Soviet Union best of all characterize the actual nature of Soviet society and the evolution of its ruling stratum.[36]

Marxism, behind the façade of women's emancipation, ridicules the traditional female role in the family as 'galley labour', but does so for the purpose of delivering women to the 'galley labour' of the Marxist state. The Marxist solution is to take the child from the parents and substitute parental authority for the State via childcare. As is apparent today, the Marxist ideal regarding the family and children is the same as that of big capitalism. It is typical of the manner by which Marxism, including Communism, converges with plutocracy, as Spengler pointed out soon after the 1917 Revolution in Russia.[37]

Trotsky states, 'you cannot "abolish" the family; you have to replace it'. The aim was to replace the family with the state apparatus: 'During the lean years, the workers wherever possible, and in part their families, ate in the factory and other social dining rooms, and this fact was officially regarded as a transition to a socialist form of life'. Trotsky decries the reversal by Stalin of this subversion of the family hearth: 'The fact is that from the moment of the abolition of the food-card system in 1935, all the better placed workers began to return to the home dining table'. Women as mothers and wives were returning to the home rather than being dragooned into factories, Trotsky getting increasingly vehement at these reversals of Marxism:

> Back to the family hearth! But home cooking and the home washtub, which are now half shamefacedly celebrated by orators and journalists, mean the return of the workers' wives to their pots and pans that is, to the old slavery.[38]

---

36 L Trotsky, *The Revolution Betrayed*, op. cit., 'The Thermidor in the Family'.

37 'There is no proletarian, not even a communist, movement that has not operated in the interests of money, in the directions indicated by money, and for the time permitted by money — and that without the idealist amongst its leaders having the slightest suspicion of the fact'. Oswald Spengler, *The Decline of The West* (London: George Allen and Unwin, 1971),Vol. II, 402.

38 L Trotsky, op.cit.

The original Bolshevik plan was for a new slavery where all would be bound to the factory floor regardless of gender, a now familiar aim of global capitalism, behind the façade of 'equality'. Trotsky lamented that the rural family was even stronger: 'The rural family, bound up not only with home industry but with agriculture, is infinitely more stable and conservative than that of the town'. There had been major reversals in the collectivisation of the peasant families: they were again obtaining most of their food from private lots rather than collectivised farms, and 'there can no longer be any talk of social dining rooms'. 'Thus the midget farms, [we're] creating a new basis for the domestic hearthstone[39]

The pioneering of abortion rights by the Leninist regime was celebrated as a great achievement of Bolshevism, which was, however, reversed by Stalin with the celebration instead of motherhood. In terms that are today conventional throughout the Western world, Trotsky stated that due to the economic burden of children upon women:

> ...It is just for this reason that the revolutionary power gave women the right to abortion, which in conditions of want and family distress, whatever may be said upon this subject by the eunuchs and old maids of both sexes, is one of her most important civil, political and cultural rights. However, this right of women too, gloomy enough in itself, is under the existing social inequality being converted into a privilege.[40]

The Old Bolsheviks demanded abortion as a means of 'emancipating women' from children and family. One can hardly account for the Bolshevik attitude by an appeal to anyone's 'rights' (sic). The answer to the economic hardship of childbearing was surely to eliminate the causes of the hardship. In fact, this was the aim of the Stalinists, Trotsky citing this in condemnation:

> One of the members of the highest Soviet court, Soltz, a specialist on matrimonial questions, bases the forthcoming

---

39   *Ibid.*
40   *Ibid.*

prohibition of abortion on the fact that in a socialist society where there are no unemployed, etc., etc., a woman has no right to decline 'the joys of motherhood'.[41]

On June 27 1936 a law was passed prohibiting abortion, which Trotsky called the natural and logical fruit of a 'Thermidorian reaction'.[42] The redemption of the family and motherhood was damned perhaps more vehemently by Trotsky than any other aspect of Stalinism as a repudiation of the 'ABCs of Communism', which he stated includes 'getting women out of the clutches of the family'.

> Everybody and everything is dragged into the new course: lawgiver and litterateur, court and militia, newspaper and schoolroom. When a naive and honest communist youth makes bold to write in his paper: 'You would do better to occupy yourself with solving the problem how woman can get out of the clutches of the family', he receives in answer a couple of good smacks and – is silent. The ABCs of Communism are declared a 'leftist excess'. The stupid and stale prejudices of uncultured philistines are resurrected in the name of a new morale. And what is happening in daily life in all the nooks and corners of this measureless country? The press reflects only in a faint degree the depth of the Thermidorian reaction in the sphere of the family.[43]

A 'new' or what we might better call traditional 'morale' had returned. Marriage and family were being revived in contrast to the laws of early Bolshevik rule:

> The lyric, academical and other 'friends of the Soviet Union' have eyes in order to see nothing. The marriage and family laws established by the October revolution, once the object of its legitimate pride, are being made over and mutilated by vast borrowings from the law treasuries of the bourgeois countries. And as though on purpose to stamp treachery

---

41   *Ibid.*
42   *Ibid.*
43   *Ibid.*

with ridicule, the same arguments which were earlier advanced in favor of unconditional freedom of divorce and abortion – 'the liberation of women', 'defense of the rights of personality', 'protection of motherhood' – are repeated now in favor of their limitation and complete prohibition.[44]

Trotsky proudly stated that the Bolsheviks had sought to alienate children from their parents, but under Stalin parents resumed their responsibilities as the guardians of their children's welfare, rather than the role being allotted to factory crèches. It seems, that in this respect at least, Stalinist Russia was less a Marxian-Bolshevik state than the present day capitalist states which insist that mothers should leave their children to the upbringing of crèches while they are forced to work; and ironically those most vocal in demanding such policies are often regarded as 'right-wing'.

Trotsky lauded the policy of the early Bolshevik state, to the point where the state withdrew support from parents

> While the hope still lived of concentrating the education of the new generations in the hands of the state, the government was not only unconcerned about supporting the authority of the 'elders', and, in particular of the mother and father, but on the contrary tried its best to separate the children from the family, in order thus to protect them from the traditions of a stagnant mode of life.[45]

Trotsky portrayed the early Bolshevik experiments as the saving of children from 'drunken fathers or religious mothers'; 'a shaking of parental authority to its very foundations'.[46]

Stalinist Russia also reversed the original Bolshevik education policy that had been based on 'progressive' American concepts and returned authority to the schools. In speaking of the campaign against decadence in music,[47] Andrei Zhdanov, Stalin's cultural

---

44   *Ibid.*
45   *Ibid.*
46   *Ibid.*
47   See below.

adviser, recalled the original Bolshevik education policy, and disparaged it as 'very leftish':

At one time, you remember, elementary and secondary schools went in for the 'laboratory brigade' method and the 'Dalton plan',[48] which reduced the role of the teacher in the schools to a minimum and gave each pupil the right to set the theme of classwork at the beginning of each lesson. On arriving in the classroom, the teacher would ask the pupils 'What shall we study today?' The pupils would reply: 'Tell us about the Arctic', 'Tell us about the Antarctic', 'Tell us about Chapayev', 'Tell us about Dneprostroi'. The teacher had to follow the lead of these demands. This was called the 'laboratory brigade method', but actually it amounted to turning the organisation of schooling completely topsy-turvy. The pupils became the directing force, and the teacher followed their lead. Once we had 'loose-leaf textbooks', and the five point system of marks was abandoned. All these things were novelties, but I ask you, did these novelties stand for progress?

The Party cancelled all these 'novelties', as you know. Why? Because these 'novelties', in form very 'leftish', were in actual fact extremely reactionary and made for the nullification of the school.[49]

One observer visiting the USSR explained:

Theories of education were numerous. Every kind of

---

48 A laudatory article on the 'Dalton Plan' states that the Dalton School was founded in New York in 1919 and was one of the most important progressive schools of the time, the Dalton Plan being adopted across the world, including in the USSR. It is described as 'often chaotic and disorganized, but also intimate, caring, nurturing, and familial'. Interestingly it is described as a synthesis of the theories of John Dewey and Carleton Washburne. 'Dalton School', http://education.stateuniversity.com/pages/1902/Dalton-School.html

Dewey along with the Trotsky apologist Sidney Hook (later avid Cold Warrior and winner of the American Medal of Freedom from President Ronald Reagan) organised the campaign to defend Trotsky at the time of the Moscow Purges of the late 1930s. See Chapter II below.

49 A Zhdanov, Speech at the discussion on music to the Central Committee of the Communist Party SU (Bolshevik), February 1948.

educational system and experiment was tried—the Dalton Plan, the Project Method, the Brigade Laboratory and the like. Examinations were abolished and then reinstated; though with a vital difference. Examinations in the Soviet Union serve as a test for scholarship, not as a door to educational privilege.[50]

In particular the amorality inherent in Marxism was reversed under Stalinism. Richard Overy states of this process:

Changing attitudes to behaviour and social environment under Stalin went hand-in-hand with a changing attitude towards the family... Unlike family policy in the 1920s, which assumed the gradual breakdown of the conventional family unit as the state supplied education and social support of the young, and men and women sought more collective modes of daily life, social policy under Stalin reinstated the family as the central social unit, and proper parental care as the model environment for the new Soviet generation. Family policy was driven by two primary motives: to expand the birth rate and to provide a more stable social context in a period of rapid social change. Mothers were respected as heroic socialist models in their own right and motherhood was defined as a socialist duty. In 1944 medals were introduced for women who had answered the call: Motherhood medal, Second Class for five children, First Class for six; medals of Motherhood Glory in three classes for seven, eight or nine offspring, for ten or more, mothers were justly nominated Heroine Mother of the Soviet Union, and an average of 5,000 a year won this highest accolade, and a diploma from the Soviet President himself.[51]

No longer were husband and wife disparaged as the 'drunken father' and the 'religious mother', from whom the child must be 'emancipated' and placed under state jurisdiction, as Trotsky

50   Hewlett Johnson, The Socialist Sixth of the World (London: Victor Gollancz, 1939), Book IV, 'New Horizons', http://www.marxists.org/archive/johnson-hewlett/socialistsixth/ch04.htm

51   R Overy, op. cit., 255-256.

and the other Old Bolshevik reprobates attempted. Professor Overy states, rather, that 'the ideal family was defined in socialist-realist terms as large, harmonious and hardworking'. 'Free love and sexual licence', the moral nihilism encouraged by Bolshevism during its early phase, was being described in *Pravda* in 1936 as 'altogether bourgeois'.[52]

In 1934 traditional marriage was reintroduced, and wedding rings, banned since the 1920s, were again produced. The austere and depressing atmosphere of the old Bolshevik marriage ceremony was replaced with more festive and prolonged celebration. Divorce, which the Bolsheviks had made easy, causing thousands of men to leave their families, was discouraged by raising fees. Absentee fathers were obliged to pay half their earnings for the upkeep of their families. Homosexuality, decriminalised in 1922, was recriminalised in 1934. Abortion, legalised in 1920, was outlawed in 1936, with abortionists liable to imprisonment from one to three years, while women seeking termination could be fined up to 300 roubles.[53] The exception was that those with hereditary illnesses could apply for abortion.[54]

Kulturkampf

The antithesis between Marxist orthodoxy and Stalinism is nowhere better seen than in the attitudes towards the family, as related above, and culture. Andrei Zhdanov, the primary theoretician on culture in Stalinist Russia, was an inveterate opponent of 'formalism' and modernism in the arts. 'Socialist-realism', as Soviet culture was termed from 1932,[55] was formulated that year by Maxim Gorky, head of the Union of Soviet Writers.[56] It was heroic, folkish and organic. The individual artist was the conveyor of the folk-soul, in contrast to the art of Western decline, dismissively described in the USSR as 'bourgeoisie formalism'.[57]

---

52   *Ibid.*
53   *Ibid.*, 257.
54   *Ibid.*, 258.
55   *Ibid.*, 352.
56   *Ibid.*, 353.
57   *Ibid.*

The original Bolshevik vision of a mass democratic art, organised as 'Proletkult', which recruited thousands of workers to be trained as artists and writers, as one would train workers to operate a factory conveyor-belt, was replaced by the genius of the individual expressing the soul of the people. While in the West the extreme Left and its wealthy patrons championed various forms of modernism,[58] in the USSR they were marginalized at best, resulting in the suicide for example of the Russian 'Constructivist' Mayakovsky. The revitalisation of Russian-Soviet art received its primary impetus in 1946 with the launching of Zhdanovschina.[59]

The classical composers from the Czarist era, such as Tchaikovsky, Glinka sand Borodin, were revived, after being sidelined in the early years of Bolshevism in favour of modernism, as were great non-Russian composers such as Beethoven, Brahms and Schubert.[60] Maxim Gorky continued to be celebrated as 'the founder of Soviet literature and he continued to visit the USSR, despite his having moved to Fascist Italy. He returned to Russia in 1933.[61] Modernists who had been fêted in the early days of Bolshevism, such as the playwright, Nikolai Erdman, were relegated to irrelevance by the 1930s.[62] Jazz and the associated types of dancing were condemned as bourgeoisie degeneracy.[63]

Zhdanov's speech to the Central Committee of the Communist Party of the Soviet Union (Bolshevik) intended primarily to lay the foundations of Soviet music, represents one of the most cogent recent attempts to define culture. Other than some sparse references to Marx, Lenin and internationalism, the Zhdanov speech should rank alongside T S Eliot's *Notes Towards A Definition of Culture*[64] as a seminal conservative statement on culture. The Zhdanov speech also helped set the foundation for the campaign against 'rootless cosmopolitanism' that was

---

58   K R Bolton, *Revolution from Above*, op. cit., 134-143.
59   Overy, op.cit., 361.
60   *Ibid.*, 366-367.
61   *Ibid.*, 366.
62   *Ibid.*, 371.
63   *Ibid.*, 376.
64   T S Eliot, *Notes Towards the Definition of Culture* (London: Faber and Faber, 1967).

launched several years later. Zhdandov's premises for a Soviet music were based on the classical and the organic connexion with the folk, striving for excellence, and expressing lofty values, rejecting modernism as detached from folk and tradition:

> And, indeed, we are faced with a very acute, although outwardly concealed struggle between two trends in Soviet music. One trend represents the healthy, progressive principle in Soviet music, based upon recognition of the tremendous role of the classical heritage, and, in particular, the traditions of the Russian musical school, on the combination of lofty idea content in music, its truthfulness and realism, with profound, organic ties with the people and their music and songs – all this combined with a high degree of professional mastery. The other trend is that of formalism, which is alien to Soviet art, and is marked by rejection of the classical heritage under the guise of seeming novelty, by rejection of popular music, by rejection of service to the people in preference for catering to the highly individualistic emotions of a small group of select aesthetes.[65]

While some in the Proletkult, founded in 1917 were of Futurist orientation, declaring like the poet Vladimir Kirillov, for example, that 'In the name of our tomorrow, we will burn Raphael, we will destroy museums, we will trample the flowers of art', the Proletkult organisation was abolished in 1932,[66] and Soviet culture was re-established on classical foundations. Khdanov was to stress the classical heritage combined with the Russian folk traditions, as the basis for Soviet culture in his address:

> Let us examine the question of attitude towards the classical heritage, for instance. Swear as the above-mentioned composers may that they stand with both feet on the soil of the classical heritage, there is nothing to prove that the adherents of the formalistic school are perpetuating and developing the traditions of classical music. Any listener

---

65   Zhdanov, op. cit., 6.
66   Encyclopaedia of Soviet Writers, http://www.sovlit.net/bios/proletkult.html

will tell you that the work of the Soviet composers of the formalistic trend is totally unlike classical music. Classical music is characterised by its truthfulness and realism, by the ability to attain to unity of brilliant artistic form with profound content, to combine great mastery with simplicity and comprehensibility. Classical music in general, and Russian classical music in particular, are strangers to formalism and crude naturalism. They are marked by lofty idea content, based upon recognition of the musical art of the peoples as the wellspring of classical music, by profound respect and love for the people, their music and songs.[67]

Zhdanov's analysis of modernism in music and his definition of classic culture is eminently relevant for the present state of Western cultural degeneracy:

What a step back from the highroad of musical development our formalists make when, undermining the bulwarks of real music, they compose false and ugly music, permeated with idealistic emotions, alien to the wide masses of people, and catering not to the millions of Soviet people, but to the few, to a score or more of chosen ones, to the 'elite'! How this differs from Glinka, Chaikovsky, Rimsky-Korsakov, Dargomyjsky and Mussorgsky, who regarded the ability to express the spirit and character of the people in their works as the foundation of their artistic growth. Neglect of the demands of the people, their spirit and art means that the formalistic trend in music is definitely anti-popular in character.[68]

Zhdanov addressed a tendency in Russia that has thrived in The West: that of the ever new and the 'theoretical' that is supposedly so profound as to be beyond the understanding of all but depraved, pretentious or commodity-driven artistic coteries in claiming that only future generations will widely understand these artistic vanguards. However, Stalinist Russia repudiated

67   Zhdanov, op. cit., 6-7.
68   *Ibid.,* 7

the nonsense and exposed the emperor as having no clothes:

> It is simply a terrible thing if the 'theory' that 'we will be understood fifty or a hundred years hence', that 'our contemporaries may not understand us, but posterity will' is current among a certain section of Soviet composers. If this altitude has become habitual, it is a very dangerous habit.[69]

For Zhdanov, and consequently for the USSR, the classics were a folkish manifestation arising from the soul of the Russian people, rather than being dismissed in Marxian manner as merely products of bourgeoisie culture. In fact, as indicated previously, it was modernism that was regarded as a manifestation of 'bourgeois decadence'. Zhdanov castigated the modernists as elitist, aloof, or better said, alienated from the folk. On the other hand the great Russian classicists, despite their class origins, were upheld as paragons of the Russian folk culture:

> Remember how the classics felt about the needs of the people. We have begun to forget in what striking language the composers of the Big Five,[70] and the great music critic Stasov, who was affiliated with them, spoke of the popular element in music. We have begun to forget Glinka's wonderful words about the ties between the people and artists: "Music is created by the people and we artists only arrange it." We are forgetting that the great master did not stand aloof from any genres if these genres helped to bring music closer to the wide masses of people. You, on the other hand, hold aloof even from such a genre as the opera; you regard the opera as secondary, opposing it to instrumental symphony music, to say nothing of the fact that you look down on song, choral and concert music, considering it a disgrace to stoop to it and satisfy the demands of the people. Yet Mussorgsky adapted the music of the Hopak, while Glinka used the Komarinsky for one of his finest compositions. Evidently, we shall have to admit that the

---

69   *Ibid.*

70   The Big Five – a group of Russian composers during the 1860's: Balakirev, Mussorgsky, Borodin, Rimsky-Korsakov, Cui.

landlord Glinka, the official Serov and the aristocrat Stasov were more democratic than you. This is paradoxical, but it is a fact. Solemn vows that you are all for popular music are not enough. If you are, why do you make so little use of folk melodies in your musical works? Why are the defects, which were criticised long ago by Serov, when he said that 'learned', that is, professional, music was developing parallel with and independently of folk music, repeating themselves? Can we really say that our instrumental symphony music is developing in close interaction with folk music – be it song, concert or choral music? No, we cannot say that. On the contrary, a gulf has unquestionably arisen here as the result of the underestimation of folk music by our symphony composers. Let me remind you of how Serov defined his attitude to folk music. I am referring to his article *The Music of South Russian Songs* in which he said: 'Folk songs, as musical organisms, are by no means the work of individual musical talents, but the productions of a whole nation; their entire structure distinguishes them from the artificial music written in conscious imitation of previous examples, written as the products of definite schools, science, routine and reflexes. They are flowers that grow naturally in a given locale, that have appeared in the world of themselves and sprung to full beauty without the least thought of authorship or composition, and consequently, with little resemblance to the hothouse products of learned compositional activity'. That is why the naivete of creation, and that (as Gogol aptly expressed it in Dead Souls) lofty wisdom of simplicity which is the main charm and main secret of every artistic work are most strikingly manifest in them.[71]

It is notable that Zhdanov emphasised the basis of culture as an organic flowering from the nation. Of painting Zhdanov again attacked the psychotic 'leftist' influences:

Or take this example. An Academy of Fine Arts was organised not so long ago. Painting is your sister, one of

---

71 Zhdanov, op. cit., 7-8.

the muses. At one time, as you know, bourgeois influences were very strong in painting. They cropped up time and again under the most 'leftist' flags, giving themselves such tags as futurism, cubism, modernism; 'stagnant academism' was 'overthrown', and novelty proclaimed. This novelty expressed itself in insane carryings on, as for instance, when a girl was depicted with one head on forty legs, with one eye turned towards us, and the other towards Arzamas. How did all this end? In the complete crash of the 'new trend'. The Party fully restored the significance of the classical heritage of Repin, Briullov, Vereshchagin, Vasnetsov and Surikov. Did we do right in reinstating the treasures of classical painting, and routing the liquidators of painting?[72]

The extended discussion here on Russian culture under Stalin is due to the importance that the culture-war between the USSR and the USA took, having repercussions that were not only world-wide but lasting.

---

72   *Ibid.*, 12.

II

Stalinism and the Art of Rootless Cosmopolitanism

The contending outlooks of Stalinist Russia and the USA on the arts during the 'cold war' era have been referred to as the 'Cultural Cold War'. The arts were – and remain – an important part of US subversion against the traditional cultures of the world in the US bid for a 'new world order'. 'Cultural imperialism' is a primary means of imposing the 'American dream' over the world by breaking down the unique cultures of peoples and nations, to be replaced by the 'American' concepts of the 'Global Shopping Mall' and the 'Global Factory', with a uniform 'world culture', and world consumer market.

Stalinist Russia recognised the importance of the cultural question in maintaining its own cultural integrity and resisting American globalism. Stalinist Russia realised that nihilistic trends in the Left, including those within the USSR, were a corrupting influence, and worked in conjunction with America's 'Cultural Cold War'. As previously seen, Zhdanov had already launched an attack on corrupting trends in the arts, and sought to define a 'Soviet culture' that was rooted more in the folk-soul of Russia and of Europe, than in Marxist doctrine.

In 1949, the same year that America launched a decade's long world offensive in the arts, Chernov returned to and developed Zhdanov's theme, and termed cultural degeneracy 'rootless cosmopolitanism'. The term is precise in describing the character of artistic nihilism. Rootless cosmopolitans produce their art as narcissists detached – rootless - from any cultural heritage. Here, as in foreign policy, anti-Stalinist Leftists, anarchists and Trotskyites converged with the American 'Establishment' against a common enemy: the USSR. Ironically, the USSR served as a bulwark of classical Russo-European culture, purged of Leftist doctrines, while the USA promoted cultural-Bolshevism and patronised sundry extreme Left artists and art theorists, and continues to promote 'rootless cosmopolitanism' in the arts as a strategy.

Abstract Expressionism: America's 'Official' Art

Abstract Expressionism was the first specifically so-called 'American' art movement. Jackson Pollock, the central figure in Abstract Expressionism, was sponsored by the CIA's Congress for Cultural Freedom. He had worked in the Federal Artist's Project, 1938-42, along with other Leftist artists painting murals under Roosevelt's New Deal regime. Abstract Expressionism became the primary artistic strategy of the Cold War offensive against the socialist realism sponsored by the USSR from the time of Stalin. As in much else, Stalin reversed the original Bolshevik tendencies in the arts that had been experimental and as one would expect from Marxism, anti-traditional. On the other hand, American Social Realism, which had been the popular American art form until the 1930s, was by the late 1940s displaced as art critics and wealthy patrons began to promote the Abstract Expressionists.

Many of the theorists, patrons and practitioners of Abstract Expressionism were Trotskyists or other types of anti-Stalinist Leftists, who were to become the most ardent Cold Warriors. Modernist art during the Cold War became a factor in the USA foreign policy. In 1947 the US State Department organised a modernist exhibition called '*Advancing American Art*' which was intended for Europe and Latin America, reaching as far as Prague.[1]

The Trotskyites had formed an alliance with the anarchists of the modernist movement on the basis of Trotskyite condemnation of Stalinist art policy. It was a cultural offensive that was to be taken on board by the CIA, the Rockefellers and other globalists and 'rootless cosmopolitans', to use the Stalinist phrase. In 1938

---

1   Frances Stonor Saunders, *The Cultural Cold War: the CIA and the world of arts and letters* (New York: The New Press, 1999), 256.

André Breton[2], Mexican communist muralist Diego Rivera[3] and Leon Trotsky issued a manifesto entitled: *Towards a Free Revolutionary Art*[4]. The manifesto was published in the Autumn 1938 issue of *The Partisan Review*, a Marxist magazine that was of significance in the Cold War. Trotsky, according to Breton, had written the Manifesto, which states:

Insofar as it originates with an individual, insofar as it brings into play subjective talents to create something which brings about an objective enriching of culture, any philosophical, sociological, scientific or artistic discovery seems to be the fruit of a precious chance, that is to say, the manifestation, more or less spontaneous, of necessity... Specifically, we cannot remain indifferent to the intellectual conditions under which creative activity takes place, nor should we fail to pay all respect to those particular laws that govern intellectual creation.

In the contemporary world we must recognize the ever more widespread destruction of those conditions under which intellectual creation is possible... The regime of Hitler, now that it has rid Germany of all those artists

---

2   Breton was the founding father of Surrealism. Joining the Communist Party in 1927 he was expelled in 1933 because of his association with Trotsky. Breton wrote of Surrealism in 1952: 'It was in the black mirror of anarchism that surrealism first recognised itself'.

3   In Mexico Trotsky lived with Diego Rivera and then with Diego's wife the artist Frida Kahlo, having reached Mexico in 1937, where he was assassinated by a Stalinist agent in 1940.
    It is of interest that Rivera was commissioned personally by John D Rockefeller Jr to paint the mural for the RCA lobby of the prestigious Rockefeller Center, which was being constructed in 1931 as a showplace for Rockefeller power. Abby, John D Rockefeller Jr's wife, had bought Rivera's paintings for her personal collection, had Rivera's art exhibited at the Rockefeller controlled Museum of Modern Art, and had socialised with Rivera and Frida Kahlo. Nelson Rockefeller negotiated the commission with Rivera. The theme was to be: 'Man at the Crossroads Looking with Hope and High Vision to the Choosing of a New and Better Future'. With such a theme it should be obvious as to how it would be interpreted by an enthusiastic communist, whose sketch depicted a falling capitalism with the bright future of fluttering red flags and a saintly visage of Lenin. Because of press ridicule over a capitalist subsiding a piece of revolutionary art, the mural was reluctantly dismantled. Ron Chernow, *Titan: the Life of John D Rockefeller Sr* (New York: Little Brown & Co., 1998), 669-670.

4   Leon Trotsky, André Breton, Diego Rivera, Towards a Free Revolutionary Art, 25 July 1938.

whose work expressed the slightest sympathy for liberty, however superficial, has reduced those who still consent to take up pen or brush to the status of domestic servants of the regime... If reports may be believed, it is the same in the Soviet Union... True art, which is not content to play variations on ready-made models but rather insists on expressing the inner needs of man and of mankind in its time - true art is unable not to be revolutionary, not to aspire to a complete and radical reconstruction of society... We recognize that only the social revolution can sweep clean the path for a new culture. If, however, we reject all solidarity with the bureaucracy now in control of the Soviet Union it is precisely because, in our eyes, it represents, not communism, but its most treacherous and dangerous enemy...[5]

The criterion for art given here by Trotsky seems more in the nature of Breton's anarchism and of the future New Left than of the collectivist nature of Marxism. However, Trotsky, like the CIA and the wealthy American patrons of modernism, recognised the value of modernism as a method of subversion. F Chernov, whose important statement on the arts from a Stalinist viewpoint will be considered below, was to refer to such art as 'nihilism'. Given that the manifesto was published in *The Partisan Review*, which was later to receive subsidies from the CIA, Trotsky's theories provided the basis for the CIA's 'cultural cold war', and for the modernist art movement that developed as an assault upon tradition with the eager patronage of 'rootless cosmopolitan' plutocrats such as the Rockefellers and Saatchis.[6]

As Trotsky exhorted in his manifesto, this art is divorced from any cultural legacy or tradition, individualised and uprooted. There is no room for a national or ethnic culture, nor even the 'proletarian – folk – culture' that 'socialist realism' represented in Stalinist Russia, but only for cosmopolitan, nihilistic, hyper-individualised art-forms; what American conservative theorist

---

5   *Ibid.*
6   The Saatchi Gallery, London.

Wilmot Roberston called 'the atomisation of art'.[7] It is from this milieu that the CIA and the globalists recruited their agents and dupes to create their world cultural revolution.

Trotsky wrote *Towards a Free Revolutionary Art* as a call for mobilisation by artists throughout the world, an 'Artists of the World Unite!' Manifesto, to oppose on the cultural front Fascism and Stalinism, which to many Leftists and Communists are synonymous. Trotsky wrote:

> We know very well that thousands on thousands of isolated thinkers and artists are today scattered throughout the world, their voices drowned out by the loud choruses of well-disciplined liars. Hundreds of small local magazines are trying to gather youthful forces about them, seeking new paths and not subsidies. Every progressive tendency in art is destroyed by fascism as 'degenerate'. Every free creation is called 'fascist' by the Stalinists. Independent revolutionary art must now gather its forces for the struggle against reactionary persecution.[8]

The two individuals who did most to promote Abstract Expressionism were art critic Clement Greenberg, and wealthy artist and art historian Robert Motherwell[9] who was vigorous in propagandising on the subject. Greenberg was a New York Trotskyite and a long-time art critic for *The Partisan Review* and *The Nation*. He had first come to the attention of the art world with his article in *The Partisan Review*, 'Avant-Garde and Kitsch' in 1939,[10] in which he stated that art was a propaganda medium, and equally condemned the 'socialist realism' of Stalinist Russia and the volkisch art of Hitler's Germany, his criticism of Soviet art policy being consistent with the 1938 Trotsky manifesto.

---

7   Wilmot Robertson, op.cit.

8   Leon Trotsky, Breton, Rivera, 1938, op.cit.

9   'Motherwell was a member of the American Committee for Cultural Freedom', the US branch of the Congress for Cultural Freedom; as was Jackson Pollock. Frances Stonor Saunders, op.cit., 276. Both Partisan Review editors Philip Rahv and William Phillips became members of the American committee of the CCF. Saunders, *Ibid.*, 158.

10   Clement Greenberg, 'Avant-Garde and Kitsch', Partisan Review, 1939, 6:5 pp. 34-49. The essay can be read at: http://www.sharecom.ca/greenberg/kitsch.html

Greenberg was a particular enthusiast for Jackson Pollock, one of the seminal figures of Abstract Expressionism, and in a 1955 essay 'American Type Painting'[11], he lauded Abstract Expressionism as the next stage of modernism. Greenberg considered that after World War II the USA had become the guardian of 'advanced art'. On this basis Abstract Expressionism was adopted by the 'Establishment' and the CIA as a method of cultural subversion during the Cold War.

Greenberg became a founding member of the American Committee for Cultural Freedom (ACCF)[12], and was involved with ACCF 'executive policymaking'.[13] Greenberg continued his support for the Congress for Cultural Freedom even after the exposé by the NY Times and Ramparts in 1966 of CIA sponsorship of the CCF and of influential magazines such as *Encounter*. Typical of a good Trotskyite, he continued to undertake work for the US State Department and the US Department of Information. [14]

Congress for Cultural Freedom

Give me a hundred million dollars and a thousand dedicated people, and I will guarantee to generate such a wave of democratic unrest among the masses - yes, even among the soldiers - of Stalin's own empire, that all his problems for a long period of time to come will be internal. I can find the people. Professor Sidney Hook, 1949. [15]

Following the publication in *The Partisan Review* of Trotsky's *Towards a Free Revolutionary Art* the Trotskyites set up an international artists' association to build an anti-Fascist and anti-Stalinist movement among artists. This was called the FIARI

---

11   Clement Greenberg, 'American Type Painting', *Partisan Review*, Spring 1955.

12   John O'Brien, 'Introduction', *The Collected Essays and Criticism of Clement Greenberg*, (Chicago: University of Chicago Press, 1993) vol.3, xxvii.

13   *Ibid.*, xxviii.

14   *Ibid.*

15   Sydney Hook 1949, quoted on the CIA website: 'Cultural Cold War: Origins of the Congress for Cultural Freedom, 1949-50'; https://www.cia.gov/library/ center-for-the-study-of-intelligence/ kent-csi/ docs/v38i5a10p.htm#rft1

(Fédération Internationale de l'Art Révolutionnaire Indépendant). The idea for what became the Congress for Cultural Freedom after World War II, for the purposes of mobilising artists and literati behind an anti-Stalinist movement, seems to have first been created by the Trotskyites of FIARI.

The Congress for Cultural Freedom (CCF) was formally established in 1951 after several preliminary moves. The CCF had its origins in the above-mentioned American Committee for Cultural Freedom which had been organised in 1938 by Prof. Sydney Hook.[16], Hook, a leading socialist intellectual who became an outspoken proponent of US foreign policy against the USSR, and received the Congressional Medal of Freedom from President Reagan for his services, edited *The New Leader*, a socialist periodical, with his mentor, Prof. John Dewey, founder of American 'progressive education', and head of the Fabian-socialist League for Industrial Democracy. Both had instigated the so-called Dewey Commission set up in 1938 as an 'impartial enquiry' (sic) to repudiate the Moscow Trials against Trotsky, Zinoviev, Kamenev, Bukharin et al.[17] In 1948 Hook's new group, Americans for Intellectual Freedom came to the attention of the Office of Political Coordination, a newly formed branch of the CIA, directed by Cord Meyer.[18] Meyer, an internationalist, became a bitter opponent of the USSR when Stalin dashed the utopian dreams of internationalists to establish a 'new world order' after World War II.[19] Meyer was responsible for recruiting Leftists such as Gloria Steinem and psychedelic drugs guru Timothy Leary for the CIA.[20]

---

16   Hook also served as a 'contract consultant' for the CIA. Saunders, op.cit., p. 157.

17   Described by Carleton Beals, one of the Dewey Commission members who went to Mexico, ostensibly to cross-examine Trotsky as to the Stalinist allegations against him, as 'Trotsky's pink tea party', and a contrivance to exonerate Trotsky. Beals resigned amidst much acrimony from the venerable Prof. Dewey et al, but the Dewey findings exonerating Trotsky continue to be cited as the final answer to Stalin's accusations. Carleton Beals, "The Fewer Outsiders the Better: The Master Comes to Judgement," *Saturday Evening Post*, 12 June 1937. http://www.revleft.com/ vb/fewer-outsiders-better-t124508/ index.html See: Chapter III, 'The Moscow Trials'.

18   Meyer co-founded the United World Federalists with James Warburg, scion of the famous banking family, with the aim of promoting a World Government.

19   Chapter VI, 'Origins of the Cold War'.

20   'Gloria Steinem and the CIA: C.I.A. Subsidized Festival Trips: Hundreds of Students Were Sent to World Gatherings', *The New York Times*, 21 February 1967. http://www.

The founding conference of the Congress for Cultural Freedom was held at the Waldorf Astoria Hotel in 1949, as a provocation to a Soviet-sponsored peace conference at the Waldorf supported by a number of American literati. The CIA states of the CCF's founding:

> A handful of liberal and socialist writers, led by philosophy professor Sydney Hook, saw their chance to steal a little of the publicity expected for the Waldorf peace conference. A fierce ex-Communist himself, Hook was then teaching at New York University and editing a socialist magazine called *The New Leader*. Ten years earlier he and his mentor John Dewey had founded a controversial group called the Committee for Cultural Freedom, which attacked both Communism and Nazism. He now organized a similar committee to harass the peace conference in the Waldorf-Astoria.[21]

The periodical Hook was editing, *The New Leader*, was a Marxist publication whose executive editor from 1937-1961 was a Russian emigrant, Sol Levitas, a Menshevik who had been mayor of Vladivostok[22] and who had worked with the Bolshevik leaders Trotsky and Bukharin.[23] These Mensheviks and Bolsheviks became fanatically anti-Soviet,[24] with the triumph of Stalin over his political rivals. Saunders quotes Tom Braden of the CIA as stating that *The New Leader* was kept alive through subsidies that Braden gave to Levitas.[25] *Partisan Review*,[26] the Leftist magazine that had published Trotsky's art

namebase.org/steinem.html

21 CIA,https://www.cia.gov/library/center-for-the-study-of-intelligence/csi-publications/csi-studies/studies/95unclass/Warner.html

22 Myron Kolatch, 'Who We Are and Where We Came From', The New Leader, http://www.thenewleader.com/pdf/who-we-are.pdf (accessed 27 January 2010). The New Leader stopped publication as a print edition and became online in 2006.

23 Saunders, op.cit., 163.

24 Trotsky himself began as a Menshevik, the chief rival to Bolshevism after the two factions split in the Russian Social Democratic Labour Party. Trotsky then straddled both factions for much of his career, only definitively becoming a Bolshevik with the triumph of the Leninist party in November 1917.

25 Saunders, op.cit., 163.

26 Saunders describes Partisan Review as having been founded in the 1930s by 'a group of Trotskyites from City College, originating in the Communist Party front group,

manifesto, was saved from financial ruin by the Rockefeller and other Foundations and by the CIA.[27]

The CCF was able to recruit some prominent Leftists, including David Rousset, editor of Franc-Tireus[28]; and Melvin J Lasky[29], who had edited *The New Leader* and was editing Der Monat, a US sponsored newspaper in Germany, and later the influential magazine *Encounter*;[30] and Franz Borkenau, a German academic who had been the official historian of the Comintern,[31] had fallen afoul of the Communist Party as a Trotskyist, and became one of the founding members of the CCF.[32]

A socialist conference was called in Berlin in 1950 to extend the CCF into a global movement, organised by Lasky; Ruth Fischer, formerly a leader of the German Communist party who had been expelled from the party along with her faction on orders from Moscow; and the above named Franz Borkenau [33] Honorary chairmen included John Dewey and Bertrand Russell.[34] The CIA states of this conference:

Agency files reveal the true origins of the Berlin conference. Besides setting the Congress in motion,

---

the John Reed Club'. Saunders, *Ibid.*, p. 160. When Partisan Review was on the verge of bankruptcy Sidney Hook appealed for assistance, and Henry Luce, the publisher of Time, gave a grant of $10,000, while donating Time Inc. shares to the American Committee for Cultural Freedom. (Saunders, *Ibid.* 162). Partisan Review, whose editor William Phillips was cultural secretary of the American Committee of Cultural Freedom, continued to received CIA funding as did The New Leader. Saunders, *Ibid.*, 163.

27   *Ibid.*, 231.
28   *Ibid.*, 221.
29   *Ibid.*, 27-28.
30   Tunku Varadarajan, 'A Brief Encounter, Melvin Lasky is a legend. Better yet, he dislikes Maureen Dowd', *The Wall Street Journal*, 6 April , 2001, http://www. opinionjournal.com/taste/?id=90000394
31   Saunders, op.cit., 71.
32   'Franz Borkenau', Spartacus Educational, http://74.125.155.132/ search?q=cache:m2miYnAvig0J: www.spartacus.schoolnet.co.uk/SPborkenau.htm
33   Saunders, *Ibid.*, 71.
34   Russell was a patron of the CCF. Saunders, op.cit., 91. He like other Leftists and internationalists regarded Stalinist Russia as the chief obstacle to world government after World War II, to the extent that the famous 'pacific' guru advocated the atomic bombing the USSR. Russell, 'The Atomic Bomb and the Prevention of War', Bulletin of Atomic Scientists, 1 October, 1946).

the Berlin conference in 1950 helped to solidify CIA's emerging strategy of promoting the non-Communist left - the strategy that would soon become the theoretical foundation of the Agency's political operations against Communism over the next two decades.[35]

To say that the CCF and fellow-travellers were 'anti-communist', as the CIA rationalises its support, is nonsense. While the CCF and other CIA and Foundation protégés included non-communist Leftists, such as liberals, social democrats and Menshevik veterans, it is wholly inaccurate to refer to this cultural subversion as 'anti-Marxist'. The cultural offensive and the factor that united disparate elements was anti-Stalinist and such was the obsessive hatred of many Marxists, especially Trotskyites, against the USSR that they were willing to become conscious tools of the CIA and the Foundations of the wealthy. They saw Stalinism as a betrayal of Communism, to the extent of regarding US imperialism as a necessary means of fighting the Stalinists, and provided the ideological foundations for the Cold War and what continues to be mistakenly called 'Right-wing' and 'conservative'.

Stalin's Response

Around the same time that the Trotskyite-capitalist-CIA axis was planning a world cultural revolution apparently based on the Trotsky-Breton-Diego manifesto, the USSR began a cultural counter-offensive, building on Zhdanov's 1948 speech outlining a definition of 'Soviet culture' and repudiating 'leftism' in the arts.

In 1949 in the organ of the Central Committee of the Bolshevik party, F Chernov condemned the infiltration of cosmopolitanism in Soviet arts, sciences and history.[36] The article stands as a counter-manifesto not only to the Trotskyites and the 'cultural

---

35   CIA website: 'Cultural Cold War: Origins of the Congress for Cultural Freedom, 1949-50'; op.cit.

36   F Chernov, 'Bourgeois Cosmopolitanism and its reactionary role', Bolshevik: Theoretical and Political Magazine of the Central Committee of the All-Union Communist Party (Bolsheviks) ACP(B), Issue #5, 15 March 1949, 30-41.

cold war' of the time, but also as an enduring and relevant repudiation of modernism and rootless cosmopolitanism as it continues to manifest in the present age of chaos. I would go so far as to suggest that the Chernov article, despite the occasional splattering of Marxist rhetoric, and some time-specific issues, provides a perceptive critique of the modern world in accord with Conservative thinking.

Chernov began by referring to articles appearing in *Pravda* and Kultura i Zhizn ('Culture and Life'), which 'unmasked an unpatriotic group of theatre critics, of rootless cosmopolitans, who came out against Soviet patriotism, against the great cultural achievements of the Russian people and of other peoples in our country'. Chernov described this coterie as 'rootless cosmopolitans', and 'propagandists for decadent bourgeois culture', while they were 'defaming Soviet culture'. The culture of the 'West' is described as 'emaciated and decayed', a description with which any Conservative critic of Western modernism, such as the poets T S Eliot and W B Yeats or the philosopher-historian Oswald Spengler, would concur. The 'Soviet culture' referred to by Chernov is the classic 'great culture of the Russian people', and is therefore of a folkish-national character and there is nothing Marxist about it. By 1949 the highest Soviet authority – Stalin – whose views Chernov must have been conveying, had perceived that the USSR was the target of broad-ranging cultural subversion:

> Harmful and corrupting petty ideas of bourgeois cosmopolitanism were also carried over into the realms of Soviet literature, Soviet film, graphic arts, in the area of philosophy, history, economic and juridical law and so forth.[37]

It seems that these 'rootless cosmopolitans' were stupid – or arrogant and conceited – enough to believe that they were in a State that was still pursuing Marxian ideas, despite the repudiation of all the main tenets of the original Bolshevik

---

37   *Ibid.*

regime of Trotsky and Lenin. One, comrade Subotsky had, as presumably a good Marxist, sought to undermine the concept of nationality, and repudiate the idea of the heroic ethos that had become an essential ingredient of Soviet life and doctrine, especially since the 'Great Patriotic War' (World War II). Hence Chernov wrote damningly of this 'rootless cosmopolitan' whose views on culture seem suspiciously Trotskyite:

> The rootless-cosmopolitan Subotsky tried with all his might to exterminate all nationality from Soviet literature. Foaming at the mouth this cosmopolitan propagandist hurls epithets towards those Soviet writers, who want 'on the outside, in language, in details of character a positive hero to express his belonging to this or that nationality'.[38]

The USSR had become a nationalist state founded on the Russian cultural heritage, nationality and traditions; advocating nationalism and folk-culture antithetical to the internationalism and materialism of classical Marxist ideology.

Chernov continued: 'These cosmopolitan goals of Subotsky are directed against Soviet patriotism and against Party policy, which always has attached great significance to the national qualities and national traditions of peoples'.

Chernov next described an 'antipatriotic group' promoting 'national nihilism' in theatre criticism, this concept being, 'a manifestation of the antipatriotic ideology of bourgeois cosmopolitanism, disrespect for the national pride and the national dignity of peoples'.

Chernov directed his attention to individuals of a 'national nihilist' tendency in the sciences and philosophy, citing one Kedrov, who had sought to develop a 'world philosophy' devoid of 'national distinctions and features':

Here, Kedrov's cosmopolitan orientation is obvious,

---

38   *Ibid.*

advocating a scornful attitude toward the character of nations, towards their distinctive qualities, making up the contribution of nations to world culture. Denying the role of national aspect and national distinctive features in the development of science and philosophy, Kedrov spoke out for 'solidarity' with reactionary representatives of so-called stateless and classless 'universal' science. Meanwhile, the slogan 'united world science' is profitable only to our class enemies.[39]

Chernov was repudiating any notion of universalism, even in areas of science that are still generally perceived as 'universal', as belonging to everybody and nobody, such universalism being seen as a tool of the enemies of the USSR. Chernov cogently warned that 'rootless cosmopolitanism' in the name of 'international solidarity' has as its goal the 'spiritual disarmament' of the Soviet – i.e., Great Russian – people:

The forms in which bourgeois-cosmopolitan petty ideas are dragged into the area of ideology are multifarious: from concealment of better products of socialist culture to direct denigration of it; from denial of the world-historical significance of Great Russian culture and elimination of respect for its traditions to the frank propagation of servility before decadent bourgeois culture; from the spreading of national nihilism and negation of the significance of the question of priority in science to the slogan about "international solidarity" with bourgeois science and so forth and so on. But the essence of all these forms is this antipatriotism, this propaganda of bourgeois-cosmopolitan ideology setting its goal of spiritual disarmament of the Soviet people in the face of aggressive bourgeois ideology, the revival of remnants of capitalism in peoples' consciousness.[40]

Chernov identified 'rootless cosmopolitism' as part of a specific foreign agenda, which was certainly formalised that year – 1949 – with the founding of the Congress for Cultural Freedom:

39   *Ibid.*
40   *Ibid.*

In the calculation of our foreign enemies they should divert Soviet literature and culture and Soviet science from the service of the Socialist cause. They try to infect Soviet literature, science, and art with all kinds of putrid influences, to weaken in such a way these powerful linchpins of the political training of the people, the education of the Soviet people in the spirit of active service to the socialist fatherland, to communist construction.[41]

Despite the necessary allusions to 'communism', the context of the article is overtly one of Great Russian nationalism that has repudiated all notions of 'international solidarity' and 'universalism' as corrosive to the 'spiritual' health of the people, nation, state and culture, regardless of the rhetoric used. That traditional folk culture was the foundation of so-called 'Soviet culture' was explained by Chernov in referring to an episode in which the Central Committee of the party had condemned an opera, 'The Great Friendship', despite its focus on the traditional music and dances of the Caucasian folk. Stalin in particular was outraged at Muradeli for attempting 'improvements', Muradeli having composed one of the 'traditional tunes' himself.[42] According to Chernov the Central Committee resolution of 1948 had, 'subjected to a scathing denunciation the direction of some composers who had neglected the great musical legacy of the brilliant Russian composers'. The 'great Russian musical legacy' is specifically not that of dialectical materialism, or any other such Marxist notion, but clearly that of traditional folk culture, and no 'improvisations', adaptations or new interpretations were going to be acceptable. What becomes clear is that the aim of 'Soviet culture' was to create 'socialist realism' in the arts uncompromisingly founded on a bedrock of traditional folk culture. As indicated by Trotsky's art manifesto, Marxists along with liberals and globalists in the West saw something disturbingly similar between Soviet 'socialist realism' and 'Fascist' art.[43]

---

41   *Ibid.*
42   Central Committee of the All-Union Communist Party, 10 February 1948.
43   Actually, the art of Fascist Italy embraced Futurism and other modernist trends, existing side-by-side with a revival of Roman Classicism, and Italy was in this respect more tolerant of artistic innovations than Stalinist Russia. On 'Futurism' in Italy see: K R Bolton, *Artists of the Right*, 'Marinetti' (San Francisco: Counter-Currents Publishing,

Chernov was predicting what would be a major and long-lasting offensive against the Soviet, at the same time (1949) that Sidney Hook, et al, in league with the CIA, Rockefeller and other such interests, were planning to launch a world cultural revolution founded on what Stalinism was condemning as 'rootless' or 'bourgeois' cosmopolitanism'. Chernov warned of what is today called the 'cultural cold war', stating that this would be part of the 'ideological weapon' for the encirclement of the USSR:

> The most poisonous ideological weapon of the hostile capitalist encirclement is bourgeois cosmopolitanism. Consisting in part of cringing before foreign things and servility before bourgeois culture, rootless-cosmopolitanism produces special dangers, because cosmopolitanism is the ideological banner of militant international reaction, the ideal weapon in its hands for the struggle against socialism and democracy. Therefore the struggle with the ideology of cosmopolitanism, its total and definitive unmasking and overcoming acquires in the present time particular acuity and urgency.[44]

Chernov explained cosmopolitanism in terms that are thoroughly conservative and traditionalist:

> Cosmopolitanism is the negation of patriotism, its opposite. It advocates absolute apathy towards the fate of the Motherland. Cosmopolitanism denies the existence of any moral or civil obligations of people to their nation and Motherland.[45]

At the foundation of this 'rootless cosmopolitanism' is the rule of money; the worship of Mammon, and Chernov's description is again prescient as to the present nature of international capitalism or what is today called 'globalisation':

> The bourgeoisie preaches the principle that money does

2012). 32-52
44   F Chernov, op. cit.
45   *Ibid.*

not have a homeland, and that, wherever one can 'make money', wherever one may 'have a profitable business', there is his homeland. Here is the villany that bourgeois cosmopolitanism is called on to conceal, to disguise, 'to ennoble' the antipatriotic ideology of the rootless bourgeois-businessman, the huckster and the travelling salesman.

As of necessity, Chernov resorts to citing Marx in stating that 'bourgeois patriotism...degenerated into a complete sham after its financial, commercial, and industrial activity acquired a cosmopolitanist character'. Yet the Stalinist critique and cultural manifesto of Chernov is as much a repudiation of the Marxian as the plutocratic-capitalist attitudes towards nation and nationality. Marx had seen this internationalisation of capital as part of the dialectical process that would lead to the internationalisation of the proletariat, paving the way to world socialism. Marx was for that reason – dialectically – a supporter of Free Trade:

> National differences and antagonisms between peoples are daily more and more vanishing, owing to the development of the bourgeoisie, to freedom of commerce, to the world market, to uniformity in the mode of production and in the conditions of life corresponding thereto. The supremacy of the proletariat will cause them to vanish still faster...[46]

Of Free Trade Marx wrote:

> Generally speaking, the protectionist system today is conservative, whereas the Free Trade system has a destructive effect. It destroys the former nationalities, and renders the contrasts between workers and middle class more acute. In a word, the Free Trade system is precipitating the social revolution. And only in this revolutionary sense do I vote for Free Trade. [47]

---

46   Karl Marx, 'Proletarians and Communists', *The Communist Manifesto* (Moscow: Progress Publishers, 1975), 71-72.
47   Karl Marx & Friedrich Engels, 'Speech on the question of free trade delivered to the Democratic Association of Brussels at it public meeting of January 9, 1848', *Collected Works, Volume 6* (London: Lawrence & Wishart, 1976).

Contrary to Marx's dialectics, Stalinist Russia held that nationalism and patriotism are the basis upon which their socialism must be constructed. It might be rationalised that this was itself a dialectical process for the eventual establishment of the world communist society in which all nations would disappear including the Russian. Yet the exhortation of the Stalinists for loyalty to the 'Socialist Motherland' was based on a nationalism which was stridently folkish and made the 'Great Russians' a unique nationality, not because they were citizens of the first 'Socialist state' or any other such nebulous ideological formulae, but due to what Chernov described in un-Marxian terms as their innate and superior characteristics.

Chernov cogently stated precisely the agenda of the 'cultural cold warriors' that was about to emerge from the USA: 'In the era of imperialism the ideology of cosmopolitanism is a weapon in the struggle of imperialist plunderers seeking world domination'.[48] And so it remains, as will be outlined in the concluding paragraphs.

If any doubt remained as to what Chernov meant by nationalism as the bulwark against international capital, and that Stalinism was an explicit repudiation of Marxist notions of internationalism despite Chernov's necessary ideological allusions to Lenin, Chernov makes it plain that it is precisely the type of nationalism condemned by Marx that was nonetheless the foundation of the Soviet State of the Great Russians:

> National sovereignty, the struggle of oppressed nations for their liberation, the patriotic feelings of freedom-loving peoples and above all the mighty patriotism of the Soviet people - these still serve as a serious obstacle for predatory imperialistic aspirations, they prevent the imperialists' accomplishing their plans of establishing world-wide domination. Seeking to crush the peoples' will for resistance, the imperialist bourgeoisie and their agents in the camp of Right-wing socialists preach that national

---

48   F Chernov, op. cit.

sovereignty purportedly became obsolete and a thing past its time, they proclaim the fiction of the very notion of nation and state independence.[49]

If Chernov and even Stalin had been free to express themselves outside the bounds of Marxism-Leninist rhetoric they could have added that Marx himself was among those who – like the 'predatory imperialists' – preached that 'national sovereignty was obsolete'. Those who did follow the Marxist line of 'rootless cosmopolitism', such as the Trotskyites, were then teaming up with the 'predatory imperialists' in the USA and elsewhere to launch their offensive against the USSR: 'The ruling cliques of nations, being the objects of American expansion go all out so as to spit upon and fault the yearning of the masses for the preservation of their national sovereignty, thus rendering aid to American imperialism'.[50]

Chernov showed that the USSR and the Soviet bloc considered their own historic mission not as the centre for 'world revolution', the ideal of the Trotskyites, but as the bulwark against one-worldism:

> In the guise of cosmopolitan phraseology, in false slogans about the struggle against 'nationalist selfishness', hides the brutal face of the inciters of a new war, trying to bring about the fantastic notion of American rule over the world. From the imperialist circles of the USA today issues propaganda of 'world citizenship' and 'universal government'.[51]

The above passage must be put into the context of the 'Cold War' that was emerging, as the result of Stalin's rejection of the US demand for a United Nations as the vehicle for 'universal government', and the Soviet repudiation of the 'Baruch Plan' which would have given such a 'universal government' control

---

49   F. Chernov, op.cit.
50   *Ibid.*
51   *Ibid.*

over atomic energy.[52] Indeed, if the reader did not realise that the above passage was written by a Soviet functionary, would it not be assumed to be the statement of a 'right-wing extremist'? Chernov continued, drawing on the 1948 speech of Zhdanov: 'Comrade A A Zhdanov showed that bourgeois cosmopolitism and, in particular, the cosmopolitan idea of "one-world government" have a strikingly expressed anti-Soviet orientation'.[53]

Rockefeller Sponsorship of Rootless Cosmopolitanism

This was the background against which the 'cultural cold war' was formulated: that of a Trotskyite-liberal-plutocratic alliance against an intransigently nationalistic USSR that had rejected firstly the 'world revolution' of Trotsky, and secondly the 'one-world government' proposed by the USA in the aftermath World War II.

The leading patron of American Modernism has been the Rockefeller founded and owned Museum of Modern Art (MoMA).[54] John J Whitney, formerly of the US Government's Psychological Strategy Board, was a trustee of the Museum, and he supported Jackson Pollock and other modernists.[55] According to the archives of the Rockefeller Center, Abby, Nelson and David Rockefeller were particularly important to the 'founding and continuous success of the museum'.[56]

Abby Rockefeller had co-founded MoMA in 1929. Her son Nelson had been museum president through the 1940s and 1950s.[57] Nelson was an enthusiastic promoter of Abstract Expressionism, and described it as 'free enterprise painting',[58] while others promoted it because of its revolutionary socialist virtues. Nelson Rockefeller became president of the Museum

---

52   See: Chapter V, 'Origins of the Cold War'.
53   F Chernov, op. cit.
54   Saunders, op cit., 257.
55   Ibid., 263.
56   Research Reports from the Rockefeller Archive Center, Spring, 1997.
57   Saunders, op.cit., 257.
58   Ibid., 258.

in 1939[59]. After his service as Assistant Secretary of State for Latin America, he resumed the role in 1946. While Nelson was Coordinator of Inter-American Affairs, the Department organised exhibitions of 'contemporary American painting', nineteen of which were contracted to the MoMA.[60] He was closely linked with the CIA, according to Tom Braden.[61] In 1954 Nelson became President Eisenhower's special adviser on Cold War policy. [62]

John Whitney was a MoMA Trustee, while also serving as chairman and president of the board. He had served with the CIA-forerunner, the OSS during the war, after which he continued to work with the CIA. William Burden, who joined the museum as chairman of its Advisory Committee in 1940, worked with Nelson Rockefeller's Latin American Department during the war. A 'venture capitalist' like Whitney, he had been president of the CIA's Farfield Foundation; and in 1947 was appointed chairman of the Committee on Museum Collections, and in 1956 as MoMA's president.[63] Other corporate trustees of MoMA were William Paley, owner of CBS, and Henry Luce of Time-Life Inc., who both assisted the CIA.[64] Joseph Reed, Gardner Cowles, Junkie Fleischmann, and Cass Canfield were all simultaneously trustees of MoMA and of the CIA's Farfield Foundation. There were numerous other connections between the CIA and the museum, including that of Tom Braden, who had been executive secretary of the museum through 1947-1949 before joining the CIA.[65] Clearly MoMA has long been considered a major element in the globalist strategy for a 'new world order'.

In 1952 MoMA launched its world revolution of Abstract Expressionism via the International Program. This received a

---

59   *Ibid.*, 257.
60   Saunder, op.cit., 260.
61   *Ibid.*, 261.
62   *Ibid.*
63   *Ibid.*
64   *Ibid.*, 262. Luce's Life magazine featured Jackson Pollock in its August 1949 issue, giving Pollock household fame. Saunders, *Ibid.*, 267.
65   *Ibid.*, 263.

five year annual grant of $125,000 from the Rockefeller Brothers Fund, under the direction of Porter McCray, who had also worked with Nelson's Latin American Department, and in 1950 as an attaché of the cultural section of the US Foreign Service.[66] Russell Lynes, writing of this period stated that MoMA now had the entire world to 'proselytise' with what he called 'the exportable religion' of Abstract Expressionism[67].

While the CIA's Congress for Cultural Freedom no longer exists, the cultural-bolshevism it was set up to promote set the trend for a nihilism that has not abated in the world of the Arts, but has rather accelerated. All criteria for what constitutes art and culture generally has been rendered redundant, and derided as 'old fashioned' and 'reactionary', while Modernism remains a tool for those who see the Arts as a means of creating a universal 'culture' as the basis for a 'universal state', or 'new world order' as it is now called. Chernov's Stalinist analysis of the arts in 1949 predicted what would take place.

Despite the fall of the Soviet bloc and the end of the Cold War there has been no cessation of the globalist cultural offensive. The National Endowment for Democracy was formed by neo-Trotskyites with the help of neo-conservatives and funding from US Congress to assume the role of the CIA and CCF in instigating global subversion.[68] A new 'Cold War' era was declared with the so-called 'war on terrorism'. With the destruction of the Soviet bloc a new was bogey was invented: 'Islamofascism', a term coined by Trotskyite-turned neo-con, Stephen Schwartz, Director of the Center for Islamic Pluralism; thereby making Islam the new Stalinism/Hitlerism.[69] Like World War II, this

---

66 *Ibid.*, 267.

67 Russell Lynes, *Good Old Modern Art: An Intimidate Portrait of the Museum of Modern Art* (New York: Atheneum, 1973), cited by Saunders, op.cit., 267.

68 The National Endowment for Democracy was established in 1983 by Act of US Congress, at the prompting of Tom Kahn, an adherent of the Shachtmanite wing of US Trotskyism; which has supported US foreign policy since the Cold War.

69 Schwartz was a supporter of the Trotskyist Fomento Obrero Revolucionario during the 1930s. Like possibly most Trotskyists of note he ended up as a 'neo-conservative' (which is neither 'new' nor 'conservative'), and writes as a columnist for National Review; a phenomenon that would not have surprised Stalin. Schwartz affirmed that, 'To my last breath I will defend Trotsky... The Shachtmanites, in the 1960s, joined the

new era of tension is supposed to herald a one world government or what President George H W Bush referred to as a 'new world order'. Again, Russia threw a spanner in the works, and the post-Yeltsin regime under Putin has been uncooperative, while the globalists warn of an ominous return to Stalinism in Russia.

The cultural offensive is being continued as a primary strategy for the 'emaciation'[70] of nations, cultures and peoples. America as the historic centre of world Bolshevism has its own version of Trotsky's 'permanent revolution' which US strategists call 'constant conflict'. Major Ralph Peters[71], a prominent military strategist, appears to have coined the term. Peters has written of this in an article by that name:

We have entered an age of constant conflict. …

We are entering a new American century, in which we will become still wealthier, culturally more lethal, and increasingly powerful. We will excite hatreds without precedent.

Information destroys traditional jobs and traditional cultures; it seduces, betrays, yet remains invulnerable. How can you counterattack the information others have turned upon you? There is no effective option other than

---

AFL-CIO in its best Cold War period, and many became staunch Reaganites'. Stephen Schwartz, 'Trotskycons?,' National Review, 11 June 2003: http://faceoff.nationalreview. com/comment/comment-schwartz061103.asp

70   Chernov, op.cit.

71   Peters was assigned to the Office of the Deputy Chief of Staff for Intelligence, where he was responsible for future warfare. Prior to becoming a Foreign Area Officer for Eurasia, he served exclusively at the tactical level. He is a graduate of the US Army Command and General Staff College. Over the past several years, his professional and personal research took Peters to Russia, Ukraine, Georgia, Ossetia, Abkhazia, Armenia, Azerbaijan, Uzbekistan, Kazakhstan, Latvia, Lithuania, Estonia, Croatia, Serbia, Bulgaria, Romania, Poland, Hungary, the Czech Republic, Pakistan, Turkey, Burma, Laos, Thailand, and Mexico, as well as the countries of the Andean Ridge. He has published widely on military and international concerns. Peters retired in 1998 with the rank of Lieutenant Colonel, and continues to write widely as a novelist, essayist and is a frequent media commentator. Peters' primary area of expertise appears to be Eurasia and the former Soviet bloc states, those states that are particularly targeted by the 'colour revolutions' instigated by the National Endowment for Democracy, and others.

competitive performance. For those individuals and cultures that cannot join or compete with our information empire, there is only inevitable failure ...The attempt of the Iranian mullahs to secede from modernity has failed, although a turbaned corpse still stumbles about the neighborhood. Information, from the internet to rock videos, will not be contained, and fundamentalism cannot control its children. Our victims volunteer.[72]

Peters is stating that this 'global information empire' led by the USA is 'historically inevitable'. This 'historical inevitability' is classic Karl Marx, just as 'constant conflict' is classic Trotsky. This is a 'cultural revolution', which is buttressed by American firepower. Peters continues:

It is fashionable among world intellectual elites to decry 'American culture', with our domestic critics among the loudest in complaint. But traditional intellectual elites are of shrinking relevance, replaced by cognitive-practical elites — figures such as Bill Gates, Steven Spielberg, Madonna, or our most successful politicians — human beings who can recognize or create popular appetites, recreating themselves as necessary. Contemporary American culture is the most powerful in history, and the most destructive of competitor cultures. While some other cultures, such as those of East Asia, appear strong enough to survive the onslaught by adaptive behaviours, most are not. The genius, the secret weapon, of American culture is the essence that the elites despise: ours is the first genuine people's culture. It stresses comfort and convenience — ease — and it generates pleasure for the masses. We are Karl Marx's dream, and his nightmare.[73]

Peters' enthusiastic messianic prophecies for the 'American Century' are reminiscent of Huxley's *Brave New World* where the masses are kept in servitude not by physical force but by

---

72   Ralph Peters, 'Constant Conflict', Parameters, Summer 1997, 4-14. http://www.usamhi.
      army.mil/USAWC/Parameters/97summer/peters.htm
73   *Ibid.*

mindless narcosis, but addiction to the puerile,[74] everything that is in a word 'American' in the modern sense.

> Secular and religious revolutionaries in our century have made the identical mistake, imagining that the workers of the world or the faithful just can't wait to go home at night to study Marx or the Koran. Well, Joe Sixpack, Ivan Tipichni, and Ali Quat would rather 'Baywatch.' America has figured it out, and we are brilliant at operationalizing our knowledge, and our cultural power will hinder even those cultures we do not undermine. There is no 'peer competitor' in the cultural (or military) department. Our cultural empire has the addicted — men and women everywhere — clamoring for more. And they pay for the privilege of their disillusionment.[75]

The 'constant conflict' is one of world cultural revolution, with the armed forces used as backup against any reticent state. The world is therefore to be kept in a permanent state of flux, with a lack of permanence, which Peters' calls Americas' 'strength', as settled traditional modes of life do not accord with the aim of infinite industrial, technical and economic 'progress'. Peters:

> There will be no peace. At any given moment for the rest of our lifetimes, there will be multiple conflicts in mutating forms around the globe. Violent conflict will dominate the headlines, but cultural and economic struggles will be steadier and ultimately more decisive. The de facto role of the US armed forces will be to keep the world safe for our economy and open to our cultural assault. To those ends, we will do a fair amount of killing.[76]

Peters refers to certain cultures trying to reassert their traditions, and again emphasises that the globalist 'culture' that is being imposed is one of a Huxleyan 'infectious pleasure'. The historical inevitability is re-emphasised, as the 'rejectionist' (sic) regimes

---

74 K R Bolton, *Revolution from Above*, op. cit., 'Huxley's Brave New World', 48-54.
75 R Peters, op. cit.
76 *Ibid.*

will be consigned to what Trotsky called the 'dustbin of history'.

Yes, foreign cultures are reasserting their threatened identities – usually with marginal, if any, success – and yes, they are attempting to escape our influence. But American culture is infectious, a plague of pleasure, and you don't have to die of it to be hindered or crippled in your integrity or competitiveness. The very struggle of other cultures to resist American cultural intrusion fatefully diverts their energies from the pursuit of the future. We should not fear the advent of fundamentalist or rejectionist regimes. They are simply guaranteeing their peoples' failure, while further increasing our relative strength.[77]

Michael Ledeen[78] in similar terms to that of Peters, and in neo-Trotskyist mode, calls on the USA to fulfil its 'historic mission' of 'exporting the democratic revolution' throughout the world. Like Peters, Ledeen bases this world revolution as a necessary part of the 'war on terrorism', but emphasises also that 'world revolution' is the 'historic mission' of the USA and always has been. Writing in *National Review* Ledeen states:

…[W]e are the one truly revolutionary country in the world, as we have been for more than 200 years. Creative destruction is our middle name. We do it automatically, and that is precisely why the tyrants hate us, and are driven to attack us.

Freedom is our most lethal weapon, and the oppressed peoples of the fanatic regimes are our greatest assets. They need to hear and see that we are with them, and that the Western mission is to set them free, under leaders who will respect them and preserve their freedom.

---

77   *Ibid.*
78   Ledeen is a leading member of the US foreign policy Establishment. He has been a consultant to the US National Security Council, State Department and Defense Department, and served as special adviser to US Secretary of State Alexander Haig in 1981, after having worked as an adviser for Italian Military Intelligence. He is a contributing editor to *National Review*, and a media commentator. Having been a scholar with the American Enterprise Institute, Ledeen currently works with the Foundation for Defense of Democracies, which aims for 'regime change' in states not in accord with globalism.

…[I]t is time once again to export the democratic revolution. To those who say it cannot be done, we need only point to the 1980s, when we led a global democratic revolution that toppled tyrants from Moscow to Johannesburg. Then, too, the smart folks said it could not be done, and they laughed at Ronald Reagan's chutzpah when he said that the Soviet tyrants were done for, and called on the West to think hard about the post-Communist era. We destroyed the Soviet Empire, and then walked away from our great triumph in the Third World War of the Twentieth Century. As I sadly wrote at that time, when America abandons its historic mission, our enemies take heart, grow stronger, and eventually begin to kill us again. And so they have, forcing us to take up our revolutionary burden, and bring down the despotic regimes that have made possible the hateful events of the 11th of September."[79]

Ledeen gives credit to the USA for bringing down not only the Soviet bloc, but also the white Afrikaners in South Africa, as part of the 'historic world revolutionary mission' that the USA has had since its founding. However, he states that the task of world revolution was left uncompleted, since the Third World has yet to be brought into the globalist orbit. Ledeen urged then president Bush to support revolutionary movements, such as the Northern Alliance in Afghanistan. Was the USSR ever as subversive and revolutionary in its internationalism, in its desire to impose a mono-political-cultural-socio-economic model on the entire world?

---

79   Michael Ledeen, 'Creative Destruction: How to wage a revolutionary war', *National Review* online, 20 September 2001. http://old.nationalreview.com/contributors/ ledeen092001.shtml

III

The Moscow Trials in Historical Context

Trotsky has received comparatively good press in the West, especially since World War II, when the wartime alliance with Stalin turned sour. Trotsky has been published by major corporations,[1] and is generally considered the grandfatherly figure of Bolshevism.[2] 'Uncle Joe' (as Stalin had been called by the Americans during World War II) on the other hand, was quickly demonized as a tyrant, and the 'gallant Soviet Army' that stopped the Germans at Stalingrad was turned into a threat to world freedom, when in the aftermath of World War II the USSR did not prove compliant in regard to US plans for a post-war world order.[3] However, even before the rift, basically from the beginning of the Moscow Trials of the late 1930s, Western academics such as Professor John Dewey condemned the proceedings as a brutal travesty, and a public relations campaign in the West was inaugurated in favour of Trotsky and against Stalin.

The Moscow Trials are here reconsidered within the context of the historical circumstances and of the judicial system that Trotsky and other defendants had themselves played prominent roles in establishing.

1   One of Trotsky's publishers was Secker & Warburg, London, which published the Dewey Commission's report, The Case of Leon Trotsky, in 1937. The proprietor, Fredric Warburg, became head of the British section of the Congress for Cultural Freedom. (Frances Stonor Saunders,op. cit., 111).
     Trotsky's Where is Britain going? was published in 1926 by George Allen & Unwin. His autobiography, My Life, was published by Charles Scribner's Sons, New York, 1930. Stalin: an appraisal of the man and his influence, was published posthumously in 1946 by Harpers.

2   The most salient example being the hagiographies by Isaac Deutscher, The Prophet Armed (1954), The Prophet Unarmed: Trotsky 1921-1929 (1959), and The Prophet Outcast (Oxford University Press, 1963).

3   'Origins of the Cold War: How Stalin Foiled a New World Order', Chapter V below. Russian translation: 'Origins of the Cold War', Red Star, Russian Ministry of Defense, http://www.redstar.ru/2010/09/01_09/6_01.html

A reconsideration of the Moscow Trials of the defendants Trotsky et al is important for more reasons than the purely academic. Since the scuttling of the USSR and of the Warsaw Pact by a combination of internal betrayal and of subversion undertaken by a myriad of US-based 'civil societies' and NGOs,[4] – after the Yeltsin interlude of subservience to globalisation – Russia has sought to recreate herself as a power that offers a hindrance to US global domination. A reborn Russia and a new geopolitical bloc with Russian leadership, is therefore of importance to all those throughout the world who are cynical about the prospect of a 'new world order' dominated by 'American ideals'. US foreign policy analysts, 'statesmen' (sic), opinion moulders, and lobbyists still have nightmares about Stalin and the possibility of a Stalin-type figure arising who will re-establish Russia's position in the world. For example, Putin, a 'strongman' type in Western-liberal eyes at least, has been ambivalent about the role of Stalin in history. Such ambivalence, rather than unequivocal rejection, is sufficient to make oligarchs in the USA and Russia herself, nervous. Hence, The Sunday Times, commenting on the Putin phenomena being dangerously reminiscent of Stalinism, stated:

> Joseph Stalin sent millions to their deaths during his reign of terror, and his name was taboo for decades, but the dictator is a step closer to rehabilitation after Vladimir Putin openly praised his achievements.

> The Prime Minister and former KGB agent used an appearance on national television to give credit to Stalin for making the Soviet Union an industrial superpower, and for defeating Hitler in the Second World War.

> In a verdict that will be obediently absorbed by a state bureaucracy long used to taking its cue from above, Mr Putin declared that it was 'impossible to make a judgment in general' about the man who presided over the Gulag

---

    K R Bolton, 'Mikhail Gorbachev: Globalist Super-Star,' *Foreign Policy Journal,* April 3, 2011, http://www.foreignpolicyjournal.com/2011/04/03/mikhail-gorbachev-globalist-super-star/

    Russian translation: "Mikhail Gorbachev: Globalist Super-Star," Perevodika, http://perevodika.ru/articles/18345.html

slave camps. His view contrasted sharply with that of President Medvedev, Russia's nominal leader, who has said that there is no excuse for the terror unleashed by Stalin. Mr Putin said that he had deliberately included the issue of Stalin's legacy in a marathon annual question-and-answer programme on live television, because it was being 'actively discussed' by Russians.[5]

While The Times' Halpin commented that Putin nonetheless gave the obligatory comments about the brutality of Stalin's regime, following a forceful condemnation of Stalin by Medvedev on 9 October, 2009, it is nonetheless worrying that Putin could state that positive aspects to Stalin's rule 'undoubtedly existed'. Such comments are the same as if a leading German political figure had stated that some positive aspects of Hitler 'undoubtedly existed'. The guilt complex of Stalinist tyranny is supposed to keep Russia subservient like the guilt complex over Hitler in regard to Germany. The Times article commented on Putin's opposition to Russian oligarchy, which has been presented by the Western news media as a 'human rights issue':

During the television programme, Mr Putin demonstrated his populist instincts by lashing out at Russia's billionaire class for their vulgar displays of wealth. His comments came after a scandal in Geneva, when an elderly man was critically injured in an accident after an alleged road race involving the children of wealthy Russians in a Lamborghini and three other sports cars. 'The nouveaux riches all of a sudden got rich very quickly, but they cannot manage their wealth without showing it off all the time. Yes, this is our problem,' Mr Putin said.[6]

This all seems lamentably (for the plutocrats) like a replay of what happened in Russia when Stalin deposed Trotsky after Lenin's death. Under Trotsky, the Bolshevik regime would have eagerly

---

5   Tony Halpin, 'Vladimir Putin Praises Stalin for Creating a Super Power and Winning the War', *The Sunday Times*, London, December 4, 2009, http://www.timesonline. co.uk/tol/news/world/europe/article6943477.ece

6   Tony Halpin, op. cit.

sought foreign capital.[7] As the Stalinists contended, Trotsky was an agent of foreign capital. It is after all why business, political and intelligence interests ensured Trotsky's safe passage back to Russia from New York in time for the Bolshevik coup.[8] In 1923 the omnipresent globalist think tank the Council on Foreign Relations was warning investors to hurry up and get into Soviet Russia before something went wrong,[9] which it did a few years later. Under Stalin, even Western technicians were not trusted.[10]

The purging of Trotskyites and their allies from the USSR by Stalin constituted the first significant move against foreign aims for Russia. The subsequent Russophobia that continues among American foreign policy and other influential circles has an ideological and historical framework arising to a significant extent from that period. The Moscow Trials, and the reaction symbolized by the Dewey Commission, gave impetus to a movement that was to change from Trotskyism to post-Trotskyism and ultimately to the oddly named 'neo-conservatism' (necons) and led to the formation of organisations such as the National Endowment for Democracy, working for 'regime change' around the world in the interests of the USA. In the spirit of this legacy, the oligarchs, who were unleashed on Russia after the destruction of the USSR, are being defended in the West as victims of neo-Stalinism, and their trials are being compared to those of Stalin's 'Moscow Show Trials'. Hence, American Professor Paul Gregory, a Fellow of the Hoover Institution, and co-editor of the 'Yale-Hoover Series on Stalin,

---

7   Armand Hammer, Witness to History (Kent: Coronet Books, 1987), 160. Here Hammer relates his discussion with Trotsky and how the Commissar wished to attract foreign capital. Hammer later laments that this all turned sour under Stalin.

8   Richard B Spence, 'Interrupted Journey: British Intelligence and the Arrest of Leon Trotsky, April 1917', Revolutionary Russia, 13 (1), 2000, 1-28.
     Spence, "Hidden Agendas: Spies, Lies and Intrigue Surrounding Trotsky's American Visit January-April 1917," Revolutionary Russia, Vol. 21, No. 1., 2008.

9   Peter Grosse, 'Basic Assumptions', Continuing The Inquiry: The Council on Foreign Relations from 1921 to 1996, (New York: Council on Foreign Relations, 2006). The entire book can be read online at: Council on Foreign Relations: http://www.cfr.org/about/history/cfr/index.html

10   The 1933 charges against employees of Metropolitan-Vickers, including six British engineers, accused of sabotage and espionage. M Sayers and A E Kahn, The Great Conspiracy Against Russia (London: Collett's Holdings, 1946), 181-186.

Stalinism, and Cold War', wrote of the trial of oligarch Mikhail Khodorkovsky:

> When the history of Russian justice is written fifty years from now, two landmark court cases will stand out: The death sentence of Nikolai Bukharin in his Moscow show trial of March 1938 and the second prison sentence of Mikhail Khodorkovsky expected December 27, 2010. Both processes teach the same object lesson: anyone who crosses the Kremlin will be punished without mercy. There will be no protection in the courts for the innocent, and the guilty verdict and sentence will be already predetermined behind the Kremlin walls. It also does not matter how preposterous or ludicrous the charges. Vladimir Putin was born in 1952, only one year before Stalin's death. But Stalin's system of justice was institutionalized and survived Stalin and the collapse of the Soviet Union, for use by apt pupils such as Putin...[1]

If Russia continues to take a 'wrong turn' (sic) as it is termed by the US foreign policy Establishment,[2] then we can expect the regime to be increasingly demonized[3] by being compared to that of Stalin. John McCain stated on the Floor of the US Senate, speaking of the 'New START Treaty' with Russia, that the Khodorkovsky trial indicated the flawed nature of Russia, although McCain admitted that he was 'under no illusions' that some of the gains of the oligarch might have been 'ill-gotten'.[4] However, to those who do not like the prospect of a revived Russia, Khodorkovsky became a symbol of the type of state they hoped would emerge after the demise of the USSR, and criminal oligarchs

---

1   P Gregory, 'What Paul Gregory is writing about', December 18, 2010, http://whatpaulgregoryisthinkingabout.blogspot.com/2010/12/stalin-putin-justice-bukharin.html

2   Jack Kemp, et al, Russia's Wrong Direction: What the United States Can and Should do, Independent Task Force Report no. 57 (New York: Council on Foreign Relations, 2006) xi. The entire publication can be downloaded at: http://www.cfr.org/publication/9997/

3   As was the case when Russia was condemned with Cold War-type rhetoric for going to the assistance of South Ossetia after the invasion by Georgia in 2008.

4   'Senator McCain on Khodorkovsky and US-Russia relations', Free Media Online, December 18, 2010, http://www.govoritamerika.us/rus/?p=17995

are portrayed as victims of Stalin-like injustice.[5] Trotskyite veteran Carl Gershman, founding president of the National Endowment for Democracy, used the Khodorkovsky sentencing as the primary point for condemning Russia in his summing up of the world situation for democracy in 2010, when stating that:

> As 2010 drew to a close, the backsliding accelerated with a flurry of new setbacks—notably the rigged re-sentencing of dissident entrepreneur Mikhail Khodorkovsky in Russia, the brutal repression of the political opposition in Belarus following the December 19 presidential election, and the passage of a spate of repressive new laws in Venezuela, where President Hugo Chavez assumed decree powers.[6]

Background of The Trials

The Moscow Trials comprised three events: The first trial, held in August 1936, involved 16 members of the 'Trotskyite-Kamenevite-Zinovievite-Leftist-Counter-Revolutionary Bloc'. The two main defendants were Grigory Zinoviev and Lev Kamenev. The primary accusations against the defendants were that they had, in alliance with Trotsky, been involved in the assassination of Sergey Kirov in 1934, and of plotting to kill Stalin.[7] After confessing to the charges, all were sentenced to death and executed.

The second trial in January 1937 of the 'Anti-Soviet Trotskyite-Centre' comprised 17 defendants, including Karl Radek, Yuri Piatakov and Grigory Sokolnikov, who were accused of plotting

---

5   The same situation arose with the jailing of the 'punk' female group 'Pussy Riot' for staging a filth-ridden stunt against Putin in a Russian Orthodox Cathedral, their jailing having become a cause celebre among anti-Putin interests in Russia and around the world. This is a perfect example of 'rootless cosmopolitanism' that continues to be used against Russia.

6   C Gershman, 'The Fourth Wave: Where the Middle East revolts fit in the history of democratization—and how we can support them', The New Republic, March 14, 2011. NED, http://www.ned.org/about/board/meet-our-president/archived-presentations-and-articles/the-fourth-wave

7   'The Case of the Trotskyite-Zinovievite Terrorist Centre', Heard Before the Military Collegium of the Supreme Court of the U.S.S.R., Report of Court Proceedings, 'Indictment', Moscow, August 19-24, 1936.

with Trotsky. Thirteen of the defendants were executed, and the remainder died in labour camps.

The third trial was held in 1938 against the 'Bloc of Rights and Trotskyists', with Bukharin as the chief defendant. They were accused of having planned to assassinate Lenin and Stalin in 1918, and of having plotted to dismember the USSR for the benefit of foreign powers.

These trials have been condemned as 'show trials,' yet the very openness to foreign journalists and diplomats, as distinct from secret tribunals, is surely an approach that is to be commended rather than condemned. It also indicates the confidence the Soviet authorities had in their charges against the accused, allowing the processes to be subjected to foreign scrutiny.

The world generally has come to know the Moscow Trials as a collective travesty based on torture, threats to families, and forced confessions, with the defendants in confused states, declaring their confessions of guilt by rote, as if hypnotised. The trials are considered in every sense modern-day 'witch trials'. For example, Professor Sidney Hook expressed the widely held view of the trials many years later that, 'The confessions, exacted by threats and torture, physical and psychological, whose precise nature has never been disclosed, consisted largely of alleged 'conversations about conversations.'"[8] However the opinions of first-hand observers are not unanimous in condemning the methodology of the trials. The US Ambassador to the USSR, himself a lawyer, Joseph E Davies, was to write of the trials in his memoirs published in 1945 (that is, about seven years after the Dewey Commission had supposedly proven the trials to have been a travesty):

At 12 o'clock noon accompanied by Counselor Henderson I went to this trial. Special arrangements were made for

8   Sidney Hook, 'Reader Letters: The Moscow Trials', *Commentary Magazine*, New York, August 1984, http://www.commentarymagazine.com/article/the-moscow-trials/

tickets for the Diplomatic Corps to have seats....[9] ...On both sides of the central aisle were rows of seats occupied entirely by different groups of 'workers' at each session, with the exception of a few rows in the centre of the hall reserved for correspondents, local and foreign, and for the Diplomatic Corps. The different groups of 'workers,' I am advised, were charged with the duty of taking back reports of the trials to their various organizations.[10] Davies stated that among the foreign press corps were the following representatives: Walter Duranty and Harold Denny from The New York Times, Joe Barnew and Joe Phillips from The New York Herald Tribune, Charlie Nutter or Nick Massock from Associated Press, Norman Deuel and Henry Schapiro from United Press, Jim Brown from International News, and Spencer Williams from The Manchester Guardian. The London Observer, hardly pro-Soviet, opined that: 'It is futile to think the trial was staged and the charges trumped up. The Government's case against the defendants is genuine'.[11]

Of Soviet prosecutor Andrei Vyshinsky, Davies opined that: 'the prosecutor ... conducted the case calmly and generally with admirable moderation'. Especially notable, given the subsequent claims that were made about the allegedly confused, brainwashed appearance and tone of the defendants, Davies observed: 'There was nothing unusual in the appearance of the accused. They all appeared well nourished and normal physically'.[12] A delegation of the International Association of Lawyers stated:

We consider the claim that the proceedings were summary and unlawful to be totally unfounded. The accused were given the opportunity of taking counsels.... We hereby categorically declare that the accused were sentenced quite lawfully.[13]

---

9 Joseph E. Davies, Mission to Moscow (London: Gollancz, 1942), 26.

10 Ibid., 34.

11 London Observer, August 23, 1936.

12 Davies, op. cit., 35.

13 Cited by A Vaksberg, Stalin's Prosecutor: The Life of Andrei Vyshinsky (New York: Grove Weidenfeld, 1991), 123.

In 1936 the British Labour Member of Parliament and distinguished lawyer D N Pritt KC, wrote extensively of his observations on the first Moscow Trial. In the lengthy article published in *Russia Today*, Pritt, after alluding to the good condition of the defendants who, in accord with the observations of Davies, did not appear to have suffered under Soviet detention, wrote:

> The first thing that struck me, as an English lawyer, was the almost free-and-easy demeanour of the prisoners. They all looked well; they all got up and spoke, even at length, whenever they wanted to do so (for the matter of that, they strolled out, with a guard, when they wanted to).

> The one or two witnesses who were called by the prosecution were cross-examined by the prisoners who were affected by their evidence, with the same freedom as would have been the case in England.

> The prisoners voluntarily renounced counsel; they could have had counsel without fee had they wished, but they preferred to dispense with them. And having regard to their pleas of guilty and to their own ability to speak, amounting in most cases to real eloquence, they probably did not suffer by their decision, able as some of my Moscow colleagues are.[14]

Pritt was struck by the informality of the proceedings, and commented on how the defendants could interrupt at will, in what seems to have been a freewheeling debate:

> The most striking novelty, perhaps, to an English lawyer, was the easy way in which first one and then another prisoner would intervene in the course of the examination of one of their co-defendants, without any objection from the Court or from the prosecutor, so that one got the impression of a quick and vivid debate between four people, the prosecutor

---

14   D N Pritt, 'The Moscow Trial was Fair', *Russia Today,* 1936-1937. Sloanhttp://www. marxists.org/history/international/comintern/sections/britain/pamphlets/1936/moscow-trial-fair.htm

and three prisoners, all talking together, if not actually at the same moment—a method which, whilst impossible with a jury, is certainly conducive to clearing up disputes of fact with some rapidity. [15]

Pritt's view of Vyshinsky is in accord with that of Davies, stating of the prosecutor: 'He spoke with vigour and clarity. He seldom raised his voice. He never ranted, or shouted, or thumped the table. He rarely looked at the public or played for effect'.[16] Pritt stated that the fifteen defendants[17] 'spoke without any embarrassment or hindrance'. Pritt's concluding remark states: 'But it is equally clear that the judicature and the prosecuting attorney of USSR have taken at least as great a step towards establishing their reputation among the legal systems of the modern world'.[18]

Although Pritt was not a Communist party member, he was pro-Soviet. Was he, then, capable of forming an objective, professional opinion? Anecdotal evidence suggests he was. Jeremy Murray-Brown, biographer of the Kenyan leader Jomo Kenyatta, writing to the editor of Commentary in connection with the Moscow Trials, relates that he had had discussions with Pritt in 1970, in the course of which he asked Pritt about the trials:

> His reply astonished me. 'I thought they were all guilty', he said, referring to Bukharin and his co-defendants. It was as simple as that; Pritt made no attempt at political justification, but reaffirmed what was for him a matter of clear professional judgment. …In terms of the Soviet Union's own judicial system, Pritt said, he firmly believed the defendants in the Moscow trials were guilty as charged. It was an argument which came oddly from the man who defended Kenyatta.[19]

---

15   *Ibid.*
16   *Ibid.*
17   Tomsky had committed suicide.
18   Pritt, op. cit.
19   Jeremy Murray-Brown, 'The Moscow Trials', Commentary, August 1984, http://www.commentarymagazine.com/article/the-moscow-trials/

Kenyatta, accused of being leader of the terrorist Mau Mau, whom Pritt went to Kenya to defend before a British colonial court, had been 'evasive' under cross-examination, Pritt stated.[20] Pritt, despite his support for Kenyatta, was able to judge the veracity of proceedings regardless of political bias, and had maintained his view of the Moscow trials even in 1970, when it would have been opportune, even among Soviet sympathizers, to conform to the accepted view, including the declarations of Khrushchev. Indeed, Sidney Hook, long since having become a Cold Warrior in the service of the USA, retorted:

> In reply to Jeremy Murray-Brown: the significance of D N Pritt's infamous defense of the infamous Moscow frame-up trials must be appraised in the light of Khrushchev's revelations of Stalin's crimes available to the public (outside the Soviet Union) long before Pritt's avowals to Mr Murray-Brown. Pritt cannot have been unaware of them.[21]

Of course Pritt was not unaware of Khrushchev's so-called 'revelations'. Unlike many former admirers of Stalin who found it opportune to change sides, he was simply not impressed by their veracity, and it must be assumed that his scepticism was based on both his eminent judicial experience and his first-hand observations. Certainly, Sidney Hook's leading role in the formation of the Dewey Commission for the exoneration of Trotsky, was itself a cynical travesty, as will be considered below.

If there was a general consensus that the proceedings of the Moscow Trials were legitimate, and a quite sceptical attitude towards the findings of the Dewey Commission, what has since caused an almost universal reversal of opinion? It was a change of perception in regard to Stalin in the aftermath of World War II, and not due to any sudden revelations about the Moscow Trials or about Stalin's tyranny. The wartime alliance, which, it was assumed, would endure during the post-war era,

---

20   *Ibid.*
21   Sidney Hook, *Ibid.*

instead gave way to the Cold War.[22] Such was the hatred by the Trotskyites for the USSR that they were willing to enlist in the ranks of the anti-Soviet crusade even to the extent of working for the CIA, and supporting the US in Korea and Vietnam to counter Soviet influence.[23] Their services as experienced anti-Soviet propagandists were eagerly sought by the CIA. Hence the findings of the Dewey Commission, largely ignored in their own time, are now heralded as definitive. The nature of this Dewey Commission will now be considered.

The Dewey Commission

The so-called Dewey Commission, the full title of which was the 'Preliminary Commission of Inquiry into the Charges Made Against Leon Trotsky in the Moscow Trials', having a legalistic and even official sound to it, was convened in March 1937 on the initiative of the American Committee for the Defense of Leon Trotsky as a supposedly 'impartial body'.[24] The purpose was, 'to ascertain all the available facts about the Moscow Trial proceedings in which Trotsky and his son, Leon Sedov, were the principal accused and to render a judgment based upon those facts'.[25] However, the composition of the Commission indicates that it was set up as a counter-show trial with the preconceived intention of exonerating Trotsky, and was created at the instigation of Trotsky himself.

---

22 See: Chapter V, 'Origins of the Cold War,'
23 For example, a position supported by leading US Trotskyite Max Shachtman, Shachtmanism metamorphosing into a virulent anti-Sovietism, and providing the impetus for the formation of the National Endowment for Democracy. Trotsky's widow Natalya as early into the Cold War as 1951 wrote a letter to the Executive Committee of the Fourth International and to the US Socialist Workers Party (May 9) stating that her late husband would not have supported North Korea against the USA, and that it was Stalin who was the major obstacle to world socialism. 'Out of the Shadows' *Time*, June 18, 1951. 'Natalya Trotsky breaks with the Fourth International', http://www.marxists. de/trotism/sedova/english.htm
   Given that many Trotskyites and Trotsky sympathizers such as Sidney Hook, became apologists for US foreign policy against the USSR, it might be asked whether Stalin's contention that Trotskyites would act as agents of foreign powers was prescient?
24 George Novack, '"Introduction,' The Case of Leon Trotsky', *International Socialist Review*, Vol. 29, No.4, July-August 1968, 21-26.
25 *Ibid.*

The stage was set with the founding of the American Committee for the Defense of Leon Trotsky by Professor Sidney Hook, who persuaded his mentor, Professor John Dewey, to front for it. Just how 'impartial' the Dewey Commission was might be deduced not only from its having been initiated by those sympathetic towards Trotsky, but also by a comment in a *Time* report at the occasion of Trotsky's deportation from Norway en route to Mexico: 'The American Committee for the Defense of Leon Trotsky spat accusations at the Norwegian Government last week for its "indecent and filthy" behavior in placing the Great Exile & Mme Trotsky on the Norwegian tanker Ruth…'[26]

The mock 'trial' organised by the Dewey Commission was prompted by a 'demand' from Trotsky from his new abode in Mexico, who 'publicly demanded the formation of an international commission of inquiry, since he had been deprived of any opportunity to reply to the accusations before a legally constituted court'.[27] A sub-commission was formed to travel to Mexico and to allow Trotsky to give testimony in his defence under what was supposed to include 'cross-examination'. The sub-commission comprised:

- John Dewey as chairman, described by Novack as America's foremost liberal and philosopher;

- Otto Ruehle, a German Marxist and former Reichstag Deputy;

- Alfred Rosmer, former member of the Executive Committee of the Communist International (1920-21);

- Wendelin Thomas, leader of the sailor's revolt in Germany in 1918 and a former Communist Deputy in the Reichstag; and

- Carlo Tresca, Italian-American anarchist.[28]

Other members, whose political orientations are not mentioned by Novack, were:

---

26   'Russia: Trotsky and Woe'. *Time,* January 11, 1937. http://www.time.com/time/
      magazine/article/0,9171,757254,00.html
27   Novack, op. cit.
28   Descriptions by Novack.
      See also: John Dewey, Jo Ann Boydston, John J McDermot, *John Dewey: The Later
      Works,* (Southern Illinois University, 2008), 640.

- Benjamin Stolberg, American journalist;
- Suzanne La Follette, American journalist;
- Carleton Beals, authority on Latin-American affairs;
- Edward A Ross, Professor of Sociology at the University of Wisconsin;
- John Chamberlain, former literary critic of the New York Times; and
- Francisco Zamora, Mexican journalist.

Of these, Stolberg was a supporter of the Socialist Party, described by fellow commissioner Carleton Beals as being, along with other commissioners, thoroughly under Trotsky's spell.[29] Suzanne La Follette was described by Beals as having a 'worshipful' attitude towards Trotsky.[30] Edward A Ross, who had gone to Soviet Russia in 1917 had come back with a pro-Bolshevik sentiment, writing *The Russian Bolshevik Revolution* (1921) and *The Russian Soviet Republic* (1923). John Chamberlain, a Left-leaning liberal by his own description[31], was among those who became so obsessively anti-Soviet that they ended up as avid Cold Warriors in the US camp.[32] In 1946 Chamberlain and Suzanne La Follette, along with free market guru Henry Hazlitt, founded the libertarian journal *The Freeman*. Both can therefore be regarded as among the many Trotsky-sympathizers who became apologists for American foreign policy,[33] and laid the foundation for the 'neo-con' movement. Chamberlain and La Follette continued to pursue a vigorous anti-Soviet line at the earliest stages of the Cold War.[34]

---

29   Carleton Beals, 'The Fewer Outsiders the Better: The Master Comes to Judgement', *Saturday Evening Post*, 12 June 1937. http://www.revleft.com/vb/fewer-outsiders-better-t124508/index.html.

30   *Ibid.*

31   *John Chamberlain, A Life with the Printed Word*, (Chicago: Regnery, 1982), 65.

32   Veteran British Trotskyite Tony Cliff laments of this phenomenon: 'The list of former Trotskyists who in their Stalinophobia turned into hard-line Cold War liberals is much longer'. Tony Cliff, 'The Darker the Night the Brighter the Star, 1927-1940', http://www.marxists.org/archive/cliff/works/1993/trotsky4/15-ww2.html

33   K R Bolton, 'America's 'World Revolution': Neo-Trotskyist Foundations of U.S. Foreign Policy', Foreign Policy Journal, May 3, 2010, http://www.foreignpolicyjournal.com/2010/05/03/americas-world-revolution-neo-trotskyist-foundations-of-u-s-foreign-policy/

34   *Ibid.*

Trotsky's lawyer for the Mexico hearings was Albert Goldman, who had joined the Communist Party of America on its founding in 1920. He was expelled from the party in 1933 for Trotskyism. Goldman was another Trotskyite who became a pro-US Cold Warrior.[35] The Dewey Commission's 'court reporter' (sic) was Albert M Glotzer, who had been expelled from the Communist Party USA in 1928 and with prominent American Trotskyite Max Shachtman, had founded the Communist League and subsequent factions, including the Social Democrats USA,[36] whose executive Secretary had been Carl Gershman, founding president of the National Endowment for Democracy. Glotzer had also served as Trotsky's secretary in Turkey in 1931, and had met him on other occasions.[37] The Social Democrats USA provided particular support for the Cold War hawk, Left-wing Democratic Senator Henry Jackson, and has produced other foreign policy hawks such as Elliott Abrams.

Under the façade of an 'impartial enquiry' and with a convoluted title that suggests a bona fide judicial basis, the Dewey Commission proceeded to Mexico to 'interrogate' (sic) Trotsky on the pretence of objectivity;[38] an image that was to be quickly exposed by the resignation of one of the Commissioners, Carleton Beals.

---

35   In 1950 Goldman declared himself to be a 'right-wing socialist'. In 1952 he admitted collaborating with the FBI, and stated, 'if I were younger I would gladly offer my services in Korea, or especially in Europe where I could do some good fighting the Communists'. A M Wald, *The New York Intellectuals*, (New York 1987), 287.

36   'British Trotskyism in 1931', Encyclopaedia of Trotskyism Online: Revolutionary History, http://www.marxists.org/history/etol/revhist/backiss/vol1/no1/glotzer.html Glotzer was another of the Trotskyite veterans who became an ardent defender of the USA as the bulwark against Stalinism. He was prominent in the Social Democrats USA, whose honorary president was Sidney Hook.

37   Gershman gave an eulogy at the 'Albert Glotzer Memorial Service' in 1999. http://www.ned.org/about/board/meet-our-president/archived-presentations-and-articles/albert-glotzer-memorial-service

38   John Dewey, Jo Ann Boydston, John J McDermot, op. cit., 641. Dewey is also shown here to have been in communication with American Trotskyite luminary Max Eastman.

Trotsky's Pink Tea Party: The Beals Resignation

Although one would hardly suspect it now, at the time the Dewey Commission was perceived by many as lacking credibility, despite the prestige of John Dewey. Time reported that when Dewey returned from Mexico the 'kindly, grizzled professor' told a crowd of 3,500 in Manhattan that the preliminary results of the sub-commission justified the continuation of the Commission's enquiries in the USA and elsewhere. Time offered the view that, 'by last week the committee had proved nothing at all', despite Dewey's positive spin.[39] Time, in referring to the resignation of Carleton Beals, cited him as stating that the hearings had been 'unduly influenced in Trotsky's favor', Beals having 'resigned in disgust'.[40] The Dewey report appended a statement attempting to deal with Beals.[41] In a reply to Dewey, Beals wrote in The Saturday Evening Post that despite the publicly stated intention of the enquiry to determine the innocence or guilt of Trotsky the attitudes of the sub-commission members towards Trotsky were those of reverence:

> 'I want to weep,' remarks one commissioner as we pass out into the frowzy street, 'to think of him being here.' All, including Doctor Dewey, chairman of the investigatory commission, join in the chorus of sorrow over Trotsky's fallen star - except one commissioner, who sees the pathos of human change in less personal terms.[42]

Beals observing Trotsky in action considered that, above all, his mental faculties are blurred by a consuming lust of hate for Stalin, a furious uncontrollable venom which has its counterpart in something bordering on a persecution complex - all who

---

39   'Trotsky's Trial', Time, International Section, May 17, 1937.
40   It would be a mistake nonetheless to see Time as an amiable pro-Soviet mouthpiece. Several months previously a lengthy Time article was scathing in its condemnation of the 1937 Moscow Trial and the confessions. 'Old and New Bolsheviks', Foreign News Section, Time, February 1, 1937. See also: 'Russia: Lined With Despair', Time, March 14, 1938.
41   J Dewey, et al., The Case of Leon Trotsky: Report of Hearings on the Charges Made Against Him in the Moscow Trials by the Preliminary Commission of Inquiry into the Charges Made Against Trotsky in the Moscow Trials, 'Point 6: The Resignation of Carleton Beals,' 1937. http://www.marxists.org/archive/trotsky/1937/dewey/report.htm
42   Carleton Beals, op. cit.

disagree with him are bunched in the simple formula of GPU agents, people 'corrupted by the gold of Stalin.'[43]

It is evident from Beals' comments - and Beals had no particular axe to grind - that the persona of Trotsky was far from the rational demeanour of a wronged victim. From Beals' comments Trotsky seems to have presented himself in a manner that is suggestive of the descriptions often levelled against the Stalinist judiciary, making wild accusations about the supposed Stalinist affiliations of any detractors. Beals questioned Trotsky concerning his archives, since Trotsky was making numerous references to them to prove his innocence, but Trotsky 'hems and haws'. While Trotsky denied that his archives had been purged of anything incriminating, important documents had been taken out. A primary insistence of Trotsky's defence was his denial of having any communication after 1929 with those now being tried at Moscow. However Dr J Arch Getty comments:

> Yet it is now clear that in 1932 he sent secret personal letters to former leading oppositionists Karl Radek, G. Sokolnikov, E. Preobrazhensky, and others. While the contents of these letters are unknown, it seems reasonable to believe that they involved an attempt to persuade the addressees to return to opposition.[44]

Unlike virtually all Trotsky's other letters (including even the most sensitive) no copies of these remain in the Trotsky Papers. It seems likely that they have been removed from the Papers at some time. Only the certified mail receipts remain. At his 1937 trial, Karl Radek testified that he had received a letter from Trotsky containing 'terrorist instructions', but we do not know whether this was the letter in question.[45]

It can be noted here that, as will be related below, Russian scholar Professor Rogovin, in seeking to show that the Opposition bloc

---

43 *Ibid.*
44 J Arch Getty, "Trotsky in Exile: The Founding of the Fourth International," *Soviet Studies*, Vol.38, No. 1, January 1986, 24-35.
45 Getty, *Ibid.*, Footnote 18, Trotsky Papers, 15821.

maintained an effective resistance to Stalin, also stated that a 'united anti-Stalin bloc' did form in 1932, despite Trotsky's claim at the Dewey hearings that there had been no significant contact with any of the Moscow defendants since 1929. Beals found it difficult to believe Trotsky's insistence that his contacts inside the USSR had since 1930 consisted of no more than a half dozen letters to individuals. If it was the case that Trotsky no longer had a network within the USSR then he and the Fourth International, and Trotskyism generally, must have been nothing other than bluster.[46]

Beals' less than deferential line of questioning created antagonism with the rest of the Commission. They began to change the rules of questioning without consulting him. Beals concluded by stating that either Finerty, whom he regarded as acting like Trotsky's lawyer instead of that of the Commission's counsel, resign, or he would. Suzanne LaFollette 'burst into tears' and implored Beals to apologise to Finerty, otherwise the 'great historical occasion' would be 'marred'. Beals left the room of the Mexican villa with the Commissioners chasing after him. Dewey was left to try to explain the situation to the press, while Beals countered that 'the commission's investigations were a fraud'.[47] In the concluding remarks of his article, with the subheading 'The Trial that Proved Nothing', Beals stated that:

- There had been no adequate cross-examination.
- The Trotsky archives had not been examined.
- The cross-examination was a 'scant day and a half', mostly taken up with questions about the Russian Revolution, relations with Lenin, and questions about dialectical theory.
- Most of the evidence submitted was in the form of Trotsky's articles and books, which could have been consulted at a library.

---

46 As will be shown below, Prof. Rogovin, a Trotskyite who has studied the Soviet archives, quite recently sought to show that the Trotskyites were the focus of an important Opposition bloc since 1932.

47 C Beals, op. cit.

The Commission then resumed in New York, about which Beals predicted, 'no amount of fumbling over documents in New York can correct the omissions and errors of its Mexican expedition', adding:

> From the press I learned that seven other commissions were at work in Europe, and that these would send representatives to form part of the larger commission. I was unable to find out how these European commissions had been created, who were members of them. I suspected them of being small cliques of Trotsky's own followers. I was unable to put my seal of approval on the work of our commission in Mexico. I did not wish my name used merely as a sounding board for the doctrines of Trotsky and his followers. Nor did I care to participate in the work of the larger organization, whose methods were not revealed to me, the personnel of which was still a mystery to me.
>
> Doubtless, considerable information will be scraped together. But if the Commission in Mexico is an example, the selection of the facts will be biased, and their interpretation will mean nothing if trusted to a purely pro-Trotsky clique. As for me, a sadder and wiser man, I say, a plague on both their houses.[48]

As can be seen from the last sentence of the above, Beals was not aligned to either Trotsky or Stalin. He had accepted a position with the Dewey Commission in the belief that it sought to get to the matter of the accusations against the Moscow defendants, and specifically Trotsky, in a professional manner. What Beals found was a set-up that was predetermined to exonerate Trotsky and give the 'Old Man' a podium upon which to vent his spleen against his nemesis, Stalin. It is also apparent that Trotsky attempted to detract accusations by alleging that anyone who doubted his word was in the pay of Stalin. Yet today the consensus among scholars is that Stalin contrived false allegations about Trotsky et al, and any suggestion to the contrary is met with vehemence rather than with scholarly rebuttal.

---

48   *Ibid.*

The third session of the Mexico hearings largely proceeded on the question of the relations between Trotsky, Kamenev and Zinoviev, and the formation of the Stalin-Kamenev-Zinoviev troika that ran the Soviet state when Lenin became incapacitated. The primary point was that Kamenev and Zinoviev were historically rivals of Trotsky and allies of Stalin in the jockeying for leadership. However, the Moscow testimony also deals with the split of the troika, when alliances changed and Zinoviev and Kamenev aligned with Trotsky. Trotsky in reply to a question from Goldman as to the time of the split, replied: 'It was during the preparation, the secret preparation of the split. It was in the second half of 1925. It appeared openly at the Fourteenth Congress of the Party. That was the beginning of 1926'.

Trotsky was asked to explain the origins of the Zinoviev split with Stalin and the duration of the alliance with Trotsky. This, it should be noted, was at the time of an all-out offensive against Stalin, during which, Trotsky explains in his memoirs, 'In the Autumn the Opposition even made an open sortie at the meeting of Party locals'.[49] At the time the 'New Opposition' group led by Zinoviev and Kamenev aligned with Trotsky to form the 'United Opposition'. Trotsky also stated in his memoirs that Zinoviev and Kamenev, despite being ideologically at odds with Stalin, tried to retain their influence within the party, Trotsky having been outvoted by the Bolshevik Party membership which had in a general referendum voted 740,000 to 4,000 to repudiate him:

> Zinoviev and Kamenev soon found themselves in hostile opposition to Stalin; when they tried to transfer the dispute from the trio to the Central Committee, they discovered that Stalin had a solid majority there. They accepted the basic principles of our platform. In such circumstances, it was impossible not to form a bloc with them, especially since thousands of revolutionary Leningrad workers were behind them.[50]

---

49   *Leon Trotsky, My Life* (New York: Charles Scribner's Sons, 1930), Chapter 42, 'The Last Period of Struggle within the Party,' http://www.marxists.org/archive/ trotsky/1930/mylife/ch42.htm

50   *Ibid.*

It seems disingenuous that Trotsky could subsequently claim that there could not have been a further alliance with Zinoviev and Kamenev, given that alliances were constantly changing, and that these old Bolshevik 'idealists' seem to have been thoroughgoing careerists and opportunists willing to embrace any alliance that would further their positions. Trotsky cited the report of the party Central Committee of the July 1926 meeting at which Zinoviev confessed his 'two most important mistakes', that of having opposed the October 1917 Revolution, and that of aligning with Stalin in forming the 'bureaucratic-apparatus of oppression'. Zinoviev added that Trotsky had 'warned with justice of the dangers of the deviation from the proletarian line and of the menacing growth of the apparatus regime. Yes, in the question of the bureaucratic-apparatus oppression, Trotsky was right against us'.[51]

During 1927 the alliance between Trotsky, Zinoviev and Kamenev had fallen apart as Zinoviev and Kamenev again sought to flow with the tide. The break with Trotsky came just a few weeks before Trotsky's expulsion from the Party, as the 'Zinoviev group' wanted to avoid expulsion from the Party. However all the oppositionists were expelled from the Party at the next Congress. Six months after their expulsion and exile to Siberia, Kamenev and Zinoviev reversed their position again, and they were readmitted to the Party.

During 1927 Trotsky states that many young revolutionaries came to him eager to oppose Stalin for his having betrayed the Chinese Communists by insisting they subordinate themselves to the Nationalist General Chiang Kai-shek. Trotsky claimed: 'Hundreds and thousands of revolutionaries of the new generation were grouped about us... at present there are thousands of such young revolutionaries who are augmenting their political experience by studying theory in the prisons and the exile of the Stalin regime'.[52] With this backing the opposition launched its

---

51 Verbatim Report of Central Committee, IV, 33, cited by Trotsky at the 'third session' of the Dewey Commission hearings. Trotsky alludes to this, writing: 'Zinoviev and Kamenev openly avowed that the "Trotskyists" had been right in the struggle against them ever since 1923'. Trotsky, *Ibid.*

52 *Ibid.*

offensive against Stalin's control of the Bolshevik Party:

> The leading group of the opposition faced this finale with its eyes wide open. We realized only too clearly that we could make our ideas the common property of the new generation not by diplomacy and evasions but only by an open struggle which shirked none of the practical consequences. We went to meet the inevitable debacle, confident, however, that we were paving the way for the triumph of our ideas in a more distant future.[53]

Trotsky then referred to 'illegal means' as the only method by which to force the Opposition onto the Party at the Fifteenth Congress at the end of 1927. From Trotsky's description of the tumultuous events during 1927 it is clear that this was a revolutionary situation that the opposition was trying to create to overthrow the Stalinist regime just as the October 1917 coup had overthrown Kerensky:

> Secret meetings were held in various parts of Moscow and Leningrad, attended by workers and students of both sexes.... In all, about 20,000 people attended such meetings in Moscow and Leningrad. The number was growing. The opposition cleverly prepared a huge meeting in the hall of the High Technical School, which had been occupied from within. The hall was crammed with two thousand people, while a huge crowd remained outside in the street. The attempts of the administration to stop the meeting proved ineffectual. Kamenev and I spoke for about two hours. Finally the Central Committee issued an appeal to the workers to break up the meetings of the opposition by force. This appeal was merely a screen for carefully prepared attacks on the opposition by military units under the guidance of the GPU. Stalin wanted a bloody settlement of the conflict. We gave the signal for a temporary discontinuance of the large meetings. But this was not until after the demonstration of Nov 7.[54]

---

53   *Ibid.*
54   *Ibid.*

In October 1927, the Central Executive Committee of the Bolshevik Party held its session in Leningrad, and a mass official demonstration was staged in honour of the event. Trotsky recorded that the demonstration was taken over by Zinoviev and himself and their followers by the thousands, with support from sections of the military and police. This was shortly followed by a similar event in Moscow commemorating the October 1917 Revolution, during which the Opposition infiltrated the parades. A similar attempt at a parade in Leningrad resulted in the detention of Zinoviev and Radek, but Zinoviev wrote optimistically to Trotsky that this would play into their hands. However, at the last moment, the Zinoviev group backed down in order to try and avoid expulsion from the party at the Fifteenth Congress.[55] However Trotsky admitted to having conversations with Zinoviev and Kamenev at a joint meeting at the end of 1927. Trotsky then stated that he had a final communication from Zinoviev on November 7 1927 in which Zinoviev closes: 'I admit entirely that Stalin will tomorrow circulate the most venomous "versions." We are taking steps to inform the public. Do the same. Warm greetings, Yours, G. ZINOVIEV'.[56]

As stated by Goldman, Trotsky's counsel at Mexico, the letter was addressed to Kamenev, Trotsky, and Y P Smilga. Trotsky explained that, 'Smilga is an old member of the Party, a member of the Central Committee of the Party and a member of the Opposition, of the center of the Opposition at that time'. The following questioning then took place:

Stolberg: What do you mean by the center of the Opposition? The executive committee?

Trotsky: It was an executive committee, yes, the same as a central committee.

Goldman: Of the leading comrades of the Left Opposition?

Trotsky: Yes.'[57]

---

55 *Ibid.*

56 The Case of Leon Trotsky, 'Third Session', April 12, 1937. http://www.marxists.org/archive/trotsky/1937/dewey/session03.htm

57 *Ibid.*

Trotsky stated that thereafter he had 'absolute hostility and total contempt' for those who 'capitulated', and that he wrote many articles denouncing Zinoviev and Kamenev. Goldman read from a statement by prosecutor Vyshinsky at the January 28 session of the 1937 Moscow trial:

> The Trotskyites went underground, they donned the mask of repentance and pretended that they had disarmed. Obeying the instruction of Trotsky. Pyatakov and the other leaders of this gang of criminals, pursuing a policy of duplicity, camouflaging themselves, they again penetrated into the Party, again penetrated into Soviet offices, here and there they even managed to creep into responsible positions of the state, concealing for a time, as has now been established beyond a shadow of doubt, their old Trotskyite, anti-Soviet wares in their secret apartments, together with arms, codes, passwords, connections and cadres.[58]

Trotsky in reply to a question from Goldman denied any further connection with Kamenev, Zinoviev or any of the other defendants at the Moscow Trials. However, as will be considered below, Trotsky, Kamenev and Zinoviev had formed an 'anti-Stalinist bloc in June 1932',[59] a matter only discovered after the investigations in 1935 and 1936 into the Kirov murder.

One of the features of both the first Moscow Trial of 1936 and the Dewey Commission was the allegation that defendant Holtzman, when an official for the Soviet Commissariat for Foreign Trade, had met Trotsky and his son Leon Sedov at the Hotel Bristol in Copenhagen in 1932. It is a matter that remains the focus of critique and ridicule of the Moscow Trials. For example one Trotskyite article triumphantly declares: 'Unbeknown to the prosecutors, the Hotel Bristol had been demolished in 1917! The Stalinist investigators had not done their homework'.[60] Prominent

---

58   Vyshinsky, 'Verbatim Report', 464, quoted by Goldman, The Case of Leon Trotsky, op. cit.
59   Vadim Rogovin, *1937: Stalin's Year of Terror* (Mehring Books, 1998), 63. Note: Mehring Books is a Trotskyite publishing house.
60   R Sewell, 'The Moscow Trials' (Part I), Socialist Appeal, March 2000, http://www. trotsky.net/trotsky_year/moscow_trials.html

historians continue to cite the supposed non-existence of the Hotel Bristol when Trotsky and his son were allegedly conspiring with Holtzman, as a primary example of the crass nature of the Stalinist allegations. While Trotsky confirmed that he was in Copenhagen at the time of the alleged meeting, the Dewey Commission accepted statements that the Hotel Bristol had burned down in 1917 and had never reopened. The claim had first been made by the Danish newspaper *Social-Demokraten* shortly after the death sentences of the 1936 trial had been carried out.[61] In response Arbejderbladet, the organ of the Danish Communist Party, pointed out that in 1932 the Grand Hotel was connected by an interior doorway to the café Konditori Bristol. Moreover, both the hotel and the café were owned by a husband and wife team. Arbejderbladet editor Martin Nielsen contended that a foreigner not familiar with the area would assume that he was at the Hotel Bristol.

However these factors were ignored by the Dewey Commission, and are still ignored. Instead the Commission accepted a falsely sworn affidavit by Esther and B J Field, Trotskyites, who claimed that the Bristol café was two doors away from the Grand Hotel and that there was a clear distinction between the two enterprises. Goldman, Trotsky's lawyer, had stated at the fifth session of the Dewey hearings in Mexico that despite the statements that Holtzman was forced to make at the 1936 Moscow trial that he had met Trotsky at the Hotel Bristol, and was 'put up' there, '...immediately after the trial and during the trial, when the statement, which the Commissioners can check up on, was made by him, a report came from the Social-Democratic press in Denmark that there was no such hotel as the Hotel Bristol in Copenhagen; that there was at one time a hotel by the name of Hotel Bristol, but that was burned down in 1917...'

Goldman sought to repudiate a claim by the publication Soviet Russia Today that stated that the Bristol café is not next to the Grand Hotel, and used the Field affidavit for the purpose, and that there was no entrance connecting the two, the Fields stating,

---

61   *Social-Demokraten*, September 1, 1936, 1.

As a matter of fact, we bought some candy once at the Konditori Bristol, and we can state definitely that it had no vestibule, lobby, or lounge in common with the Grand Hotel or any hotel, and it could not have been mistaken for a hotel in any way, and entrance to the hotel could not be obtained through it.[62]

The question of the Bristol Hotel was again raised the following day, at the 6th session of the Dewey hearings. Such was – and is – the importance attached to this in repudiating the Stalinist allegations as clumsy. In 2008 Sven-Eric Holström undertook some rudimentary enquiries into the matter. Consulting the 1933 street and telephone directories for Copenhagen he found that – the Field's affidavit notwithstanding - the Grand Hotel and the Bristol café were located at the same address.[63] Furthermore, photographs of the period show that the street entrance to the hotel and the café were the same and the only signage from the outside states 'Bristol'.[64] Again, contrary to the Field affidavit, diagrams of the building show that there was a lobby and internal entrance connecting the hotel and the café. Anyone walking off the street into the hotel would assume, on the basis of the signage and the common entrance, that he had walked into a hotel called Hotel Bristol. Getty states that Trotsky's papers archived at Harvard show that Holtzman, a 'former' Trotskyite, had met Sedov in Berlin in 1932 'and gave him a proposal from veteran Trotskyist Ivan Smirnov and other Left Oppositionists in the USSR for the formation of a united opposition bloc',[65] although Trotsky stated at the Dewey hearings on questioning by Goldman that he had never had any 'direct or indirect communication' with Holtzman.

If the statements of Trotsky at to the Dewey Commission and his statements in *My Life* are considered in the context of the

---

62 The Case of Leon Trotsky, Fifth Session, April 13, 1937, http://www.marxists.org/archive/trotsky/1937/dewey/session05.htm

63 Sven-Eric Holström, 'New Evidence Concerning the 'Hotel Bristol Question in the First Moscow Trial of 1936,' Cultural Logic, 2008, 6.2, 'The Copenhagen Street Directory and Telephone Directory'.

64 *Ibid.*, 6.3, 'Photographic evidence', Figure 7.

65 Getty, 1986, op. cit., 28.

allegations presented by Vyshinsky at the Moscow Trial, a number of conclusions might be suggested:

From 1925 there was a Trotsky-Zinoviev-Kamenev bloc, or an 'Opposition Centre', which Trotsky states had an 'executive committee; which functioned as an alternative party 'central committee.'

Although Zinoviev and Kamenev were aligned for a time with Stalin in a troika, they repudiated this in favour of a counter-revolutionary alliance with Trotsky, and spoke at mass demonstrations, along with others such as Radek.

Trotsky subsequently condemned Kamenev, Zinoviev et al as 'contemptible' for 'capitulating', but Zinoviev, on Trotsky's own account, was writing to him in November 1928 and warning of what he expected to be Stalin's attacks.

Was the vehemence with which Trotsky attacked Kamenev, Zinoviev and other Moscow defendants a mere ruse to throw off suspicion in regard to a united Opposition bloc, which, according to Rogovin,[66] had been formalized as an 'anti-Stalinist bloc' in 1932?

On Trotsky's own account he and Zinoviev, Kamenev, Radek, et al had been at the forefront of a vast counter-revolutionary organization that was of sufficient strength to organize mass disruptions of official events in Moscow and Leningrad, which also had support among military and police personnel.

From his exile in Siberia in 1928, Trotsky on his own account, despite the ever-watchful eye of the Soviet secret police, the GPU, made his home the centre of opposition activities.[67] Trotsky had been treated leniently in Siberian exile, and was asked to refrain from opposition activities, but responded with a defiant letter to the All-Union Communist Party and to the

---

66   See: 'Kirov Assassination' below.
67   *Trotsky, My Life*, op. cit., Chapter 43.

Executive Committee of the Communist International, in which he referred to Stalin's 'narrow faction'. He refused to renounce what he called, 'the struggle for the interests of the international proletariat...' In the letter to the Politburo dated 15 March 1933, Trotsky warned in grandiose manner:

> I consider it my duty to make one more attempt to appeal to the sense of responsibility of those who presently lead the Soviet state. You know conditions better than I. If the internal development proceeds further on its present course, catastrophe is inevitable.[68]

As a means of saving the Soviet Union from self-destruction Trotsky advocated that the Left Opposition be accepted back into the Bolshevik party as an independent political tendency that would co-exist with all other factions, while not repudiating its own programme:[69]

> Only from open and honest cooperation between the historically produced fractions, fully transforming them into tendencies in the party and eventually dissolving into it, can concrete conditions restore confidence in the leadership and resurrect the party.[70]

With the failure of the Politburo to reply to Trotsky's ultimatum, he published both the letter and a statement entitled 'An Explanation'.[71] Trotsky then cited his 'declaration' in reply to the 'ultimatum' he had received to forego oppositionist activities, to the Sixth Party Congress from his remote exile in Alma Ata. In this 'declaration' he stated what could also be interpreted as revolutionary opposition to the regime, insofar as he considered that the USSR under Stalin had become a bureaucratic state composed of a 'depraved officialdom' that was working for 'class interests hostile to the proletariat':

---

68 L Trotsky, 'A Letter to the Politburo', March 15, 1933, *Writings of Leon Trotsky (1932-33)* (New York: Pathfinder Press), 141-2.
69 *Ibid.* 'Renunciation of this programme is of course out of the question'.
70 *Ibid.*
71 'An Explanation', May 13, 1933, *Writings of Leon Trotsky* (1932-33), *Ibid.*, 235.

To demand from a revolutionary such a renunciation (of political activity, i.e., in the service of the party and the international revolution) would be possible only for a completely depraved officialdom. Only contemptible renegades would be capable of giving such a promise. I cannot alter anything in these words ... To everyone, his due. You wish to continue carrying out policies inspired by class forces hostile to the proletariat. We know our duty and we will do it to the end.[72]

The lack of reply from the Politburo in regard to Trotsky's ultimatum to accept him back into the Government resulted in Trotsky's final break with the Third - Communist - International (Comintern) and the creation of the Fourth – Trotskyite - International in rivalry with the Stalinist parties throughout the world. Trotsky declared that the Bolshevik party and those parties following the Stalinist line, as well as the Comintern now only served an 'uncontrolled bureaucracy'.[73] That his aims were something other than mass education and the acceptance of a 'tendency' within the Bolshevik party became clearer in 1933 when he wrote that, 'No normal "constitutional" ways remain to remove the ruling clique. The bureaucracy can be compelled to yield power into the hands of the proletariat only by force'.[74]

What he was advocating was a palace coup that would remove Stalin with minimal disruption. This did not mean 'an armed insurrection against the dictatorship of the proletariat but the removal of a malignant growth upon it...' These would not be 'measures of a civil war but rather the measures of a police character'.[75] The intent was unequivocal, and it appears disingenuous for Trotsky and his apologists up to the present day to insist that nothing was meant other than for Trotskyism

72 Trotsky, 'Declaration to the Sixth Party Congress', December 16, 1926, cited in *Trotsky, My Life,* op. cit., Chapter 44.

73 Trotsky, 'Nuzhno stroit' zanovo kommunistcheskie partii i International', Bulletin of the Opposition, No. 36-37, 21, July 15, 1933.

74 Trotsky, 'Klassovaya priroda sovetskogo gosudarstava', Bulletin of the Opposition, No. 36-37, October 1, 1933, 1-12. At Moscow Vyshinsky cited this article as evidence that Trotsky advocated the violent overthrow of the Soviet state. The emphasis of the word 'force' is Trotsky's.

75 *Ibid.*

to be accepted as a 'tendency' within the Bolshevik party that could debate the issues in parliamentary fashion.

If Trotsky was less than honest with the fawning Dewey Commission, the farcical 'cross examination' by the Commission's counsel was not going to expose it. Heaven forbid that Trotsky could lie to serve his own cause, and that he could be anything but a saintly figure. A less than deferential attitude toward Trotsky by Beals was sufficient to set the one objective Commissioner at loggerhead with the others.

Of the lie as a political weapon, Trotsky was explicit. Trotsky had written in 1938, the very year of the third Moscow Trial, an article chastising a grouplet of German Marxists for adhering to 'bourgeoisie' notions of morality such as truthfulness. He stated, 'that morality is a product of social development; that there is nothing invariable about it; that it serves social interests; that these interests are contradictory; that morality more than any other form of ideology has a class character'.[76]

> Norms 'obligatory upon all' become the less forceful the sharper the character assumed by the class struggle. The highest pitch of the class struggle is civil war which explodes into mid-air all moral ties between the hostile classes. ... This vacuity in the norms obligatory upon all arises from the fact that in all decisive questions people feel their class membership considerably more profoundly and more directly than their membership in "society". The norms of "obligatory" morality are in reality charged with class, that is, antagonistic content. ... Nevertheless, lying and violence "in themselves" warrant condemnation? Of

---

76 Trotsky, 'Their Morals and Ours: In Memory of Leon Sedov', *The New International*, Vol. IV, no. 6, June 1938, 163-173, http://www.marxists.org/archive/trotsky/1938/morals/morals.htm
The New International was edited by Max Shachtman, whose post-Trotskyite line laid a basis for the 'neo-con' movement and support of US foreign policy during the Cold War. CIA asset Sidney Hook was a contributor to *The New International*. (December 1934, http://www.marxists.org/history/etol/writers/hook/1934/12/hess-marx.htm; April 1936, http://www.marxists.org/history/etol/writers/hook/1936/04/feuerbach.htm). Albert Goldman, Trotsky's lawyer at the Mexico Dewey hearings, was also a contributor.

course, even as does the class society which generates them. A society without social contradictions will naturally be a society without lies and violence. However there is no way of building a bridge to that society save by revolutionary, that is, violent means. The revolution itself is a product of class society and of necessity bears its traits. From the point of view of "eternal truths' revolution is of course 'anti-moral.' ... It remains to be added that the very conception of truth and lie was born of social contradictions.[77]

Given the lengthy ideological discourse on the value of the lie and the relativity of morality, it is absurd to rely on any statement Trotsky and his followers make about anything. He lied and obfuscated to the Dewey Commission in the knowledge that he was among friends.

Kirov's Murder

The year after Trotsky's ultimatum to the Politburo (1934) the popular functionary Kirov was murdered. Trotsky's view of Kirov was not sympathetic, calling him a 'rude satrap [whose killing] does not call forth any sympathy'.[78] The consensus now seems to be that Stalin arranged for the murder of Kirov to blame the Opposition as justification for launching a murderous purge against his rivals. For example, Robert Conquest states that Kirov was a moderate and a popular rival to Stalin, whose murder was both a means of eliminating a rival and of launching a purge.[79] Not only Trotskyites and eminent historians such as Conquest share this view, but it was also implied by Khrushchev during his 1956 'secret address' to the 20th Congress of the Communist Party denouncing Stalin.[80] After Stalin's death several Soviet administrations undertook investigations to try and uncover definitive evidence against him in the Kirov murder.

---

77   *Ibid.*
78   *Ibid.*
79   R Conquest, *Stalin and the Kirov Murder* (London; 1989).
80   N S Khrushchev, "Secret Address at the Twentieth Party Congress of the Communist Party of the Soviet Union," February 1956; Henry M Christman (ed.) *Communism in Action: a documentary history* (New York: Bantam Books, 1969), 176-177.

The original source for the accusations against Stalin regarding Kirov seems to have been an anonymous 'Letter of an Old Bolshevik' published in 1937.[81] It transpired that the 'Old Bolshevik' was a Menshevik, Boris Nicolaevsky, who claimed that his information came from Bukharin when the latter was in Paris in 1936. In 1988 Bukharin's widow published a book on her late husband, in which she denied that any such discussions had taken place between Bukharin and Nicolaevsky, and considered the 'Letter' to be a 'spurious document'.[82]

In 1955 the Presidium of the Central Committee of the Communist Party commissioned P N Pospelov, the Secretary of the Central Committee, to investigate Stalinist repression. It had been the opinion of the party by this time that Stalin had been behind the murder of Kirov. Another commission of enquiry was undertaken in 1956. Neither found evidence that Stalin had a hand in the Kirov killing, but Khrushchev did not release the findings. Former foreign minister Molotov remarked of the 1956 enquiry: 'The commission concluded that Stalin was not implicated in Kirov's assassination. Khrushchev refused to have the findings published since they didn't serve his purpose'.[83]

As recently as 1989, the USSR was still making efforts to implicate Stalin, and a Politburo Commission headed by A Yakovlev was set up. The two year enquiry concluded that: 'In this affair no materials objectively support Stalin's participation or NKVD participation in the organisation and carrying out of Kirov's murder'.[84] The findings of this enquiry were not released either.

Dr J Arch Getty writes of the circumstances of the Kirov murder that the OGPU and the NKVD had infiltrated opposition groups and there had been sufficient evidence obtained to consider that

---

81   'Letter of an Old Bolshevik: The Key to the Moscow Trials', New York, 1937.

82   Anna Larina Bukharina, Nezabyvaemoe (Moscow, 1989); This I Cannot Forget (London, 1993), 276.

83   A. Resis (ed.) Molotov Remembers (Chicago: Ivan R Dee, 1993), 353.

84   A. Yakovlev, 'O dekabr'skoi tragedii 1934', Pravda, 28th January, 1991, 3, 'The Politics of Repression Revisited', in J Arch Getty and Roberta T. Manning (editors), Stalinist Terror: New Perspectives (New York, 1993), 46.

the so-called Zinovievites were engaged in dangerous underground activity. Stalin consequently regarded this group as being behind the assassin, Nikolayev. Although their former followers were being rounded up, *Pravda* announced on December 23, 1934 that there was 'insufficient evidence to try Zinoviev and Kamenev for the crime'.[85] When the trial against this bloc did occur two years later, it was after many interrogations, and was therefore no hasty process. From the interrogations relative to the Kirov assassination, Stalin found out about the continued existence of the Opposition bloc that focused partly around Zinoviev. Vadim Rogovin, a Professor at the Russian Academy of Sciences, wrote that Kamenev and Zinoviev had rejoined Trotsky and formed 'the anti-Stalinist bloc in June 1932', although Trotsky had maintained to the Dewey Commission and subsequently, that no such alliance existed and that he had nothing but contempt for Zinoviev and Kamenev. Rogovin, a Trotskyite academic having researched the Russian archives, stated:

> Only after a new wave of arrests following Kirov's assassination, after interrogations and reinterrogations of dozens of Oppositionists, did Stalin receive information about the 1932 bloc, which served as one of the main reasons for organizing the Great Purge.[86]

Hence, the primary reason for the Moscow Trials and the purge of the Opposition was found by the most recent research of Dr Rogovin, a pro-Trotsky academic, to be valid.

In 1934 Yakov Agranov, temporary head of the NKVD in Leningrad, had found connections between the assassin Nikolayev and leaders of the Leningrad Komsomol at the time of Zinoviev's authority over the city. The most prominent was I Kotolynov, whom Robert Conquest states 'had, in fact, been a real oppositionist'.[87] Kotolynov, a 'Zinovievite', was among those of the so-called 'Leningrad terrorist centre' found guilty in 1934 of the death of Kirov. The investigation had been of long

---

85 J Arch Getty, *Origins of the Great Purges: The Soviet Communist Party Reconsidered: 1933-1938* (Cambridge; 1985), 48.

86 Vadim Rogovin, *1937: Stalin's Year of Terror* (Mehring Books, 1988), 64.

87 R Conquest, *The Great Terror: Stalin's Purge of the Thirties* (London, 1973), 86.

duration and the influence of Zinoviev's followers had been established. However, there was considered to be insufficient evidence to charge Zinoviev and Kamenev.[88]

In 1935 other evidence came to light showing that Zinoviev and Kamenev were aware of the 'terrorist sentiments' in Leningrad, which they had 'inflamed'.[89] While several trials associated with the Kirov killing took place in 1935, in 1936 sufficient evidence had accrued to begin the first of the so-called Moscow Trials of the 'Trotsky - Zinoviev Terrorist Centre', including Trotsky and his son Sedov, who were tried in absentia. The defendant Sergei Mrachovsky testified that at the end of 1932 a terrorist bloc was formed between the Trotskyites and the Zinovievites, stating:

> That in the second half of 1932 the question was raised of the necessity of uniting the Trotskyite terrorist group with the Zinovievites. The question of this unification was raised by I N Smirnov... In the autumn of 1932 a letter was received from Trotsky in which he approved the decision to unite with the Zinovievites... Union must take place on the basis of terrorism, and Trotsky once again emphasised the necessity of killing Stalin, Voroshiloy and Kirov... The terrorist bloc of the Trotskyites and the Zinovievites was formed at the end of 1932.[90]

Despite the condemnation that such testimony has received from academia and media, this accords with the relatively recent findings of the Trotskyite academic Professor Rogovin, and the letter from Trotsky sent to Radek et al, in 1932, referred to by J Arch Getty. The Kirov investigations, which were a prelude to the Moscow Trials, were carefully undertaken. When there was still insufficient evidence against Trotsky, Zinoviev and Kamenev et al, this was conceded by the party press. When testimony was obtained implicating the leaders of an Opposition bloc, this testimony has transpired to have conformed to what

88   J Arch Getty, op. cit., 209.
89   *The Crime of the Zinoviev Opposition* (Moscow, 1935), 33-41.
90   Report of Court Proceedings: The Case of the Trotskyite-Zinovievite Terrorist Centre (Moscow, 1936), 41-42.

has come to light quite recently in both the Kremlin archives and the Trotsky papers at Harvard.

Rogovin's Findings

The reality of the Opposition bloc in relation to the Moscow Trials was the theme of a lecture by Professor Rogovin at Melbourne University in 1996. The motive of Rogovin was to present Trotskyism as having been an effective opposition within Stalinist Russia, and therefore he departs from the usual Trotskyite attitude of denial, stating:

> ...This myth says that virtually the entire population of the Soviet Union was reduced to a stunned silence by the terror, and either said nothing about the repression, or blindly believed in and supported the terror. This myth also claims that the victims of the repression were completely innocent of any crimes, including opposition to Stalin. They were, instead, victims of Stalin's excessive paranoia. Since there was no serious opposition to the regime of Stalin, according to this myth, the victims were not guilty of such opposition.[91]

Rogovin alludes to anti-Stalinist leaflets that were being widely distributed in the USSR as late as 1938, calling for a 'struggle against Stalin and his clique'. Rogovin also states that there was much more to the Opposition than isolated incidents of leaflet distribution:

> Of course these are isolated incidents, but prior to the unleashing of the Great Terror there was a much more widespread, more serious, and well-organised opposition to Stalinism as a regime which had veered ever more widely away from the ideals of socialism.

This battle against Stalin began back in 1923 with the formation of the Left Opposition. The inner party struggle unfolded in ever-sharper form throughout the 20s.

---

91   Vadim Rogovin, 'Stalin's Great Terror: Origins and Consequences', lecture, University of Melbourne, May 28, 1996. World Socialist Website: http://www.wsws.org/exhibits/1937/lecture1.htm

Thousands upon thousands of Communists took part in this Opposition, openly in the early days and then, after opposition groups were banned, in illegal underground forms against the abolition of party democracy by the Stalinist party clique.[92]

In 1932 the Opposition coalesced, 'the old opposition groups' became more active, and 'were joined by layers of newly-formed opposition groups'. Many representatives of the Opposition groups that year began to discuss ways of uniting into an 'anti-Stalinist bloc'. Rogovin states that the year previously Ivan Smirnov, one of the former leaders of the Left Opposition who had capitulated but then returned to the Opposition, went on an official trip to Berlin where he established contact with Trotsky's son, Leon Sedov and discussed the need to 'coordinate efforts between Trotsky and his son....' What Rogovin states is in agreement with the supposedly forced confessions of the defendants at the Moscow Trials. Getty had also found similar material in the Trotsky Papers at Harvard, previously referred to.

Rogovin states that it was only in 1935 and 1936, having assessed the information garnered from the Kirov investigation in 1934, that the secret police were able to find conclusive evidence on the existence of an anti-Stalinist bloc since 1932. 'This was one of the main factors which drove Stalin to unleash the Great Terror', states Rogovin. He also confirms the basis of the Stalinist accusations that 'they did try to establish contact among themselves and fight for the overthrow of Stalin's clique'.[93] Rogovin's statements cannot be lightly dismissed. He was speaking as a sympathiser of Trotskyism, who had access to the Soviet archives in the writing of a six volume series on the political conflicts within the Communist Party Soviet Union and the Communist International between 1922 and 1940, of which Stalin's Great Terror is volume four. On his sixtieth birthday in 1997, Rogovin received tribute from Trotskyite luminaries from Germany, Britain and the USA.[94]

---

92   *Ibid.*
93   *Ibid.*
94   http://www.wsws.org/exhibits/1937/title.htm

IV

Trotsky, Stalin and the Cold War

The Historic Ramifications of the Trotsky-Stalin Conflict

The Moscow Trials were symptomatic of a great divide that had occurred in Bolshevism. The alliance with Stalin during World War II had formed an assumption among US internationalists that after the Axis defeat a 'new world order' would emerge via the United Nations Organisation. This assumption was ill-founded, and the result was the Cold War. Trotskyists emerged as avid Cold Warriors dialectically concluding that the USSR represented the primary obstacle to world socialism. This chapter examines the dialectical process by which major factions of Trotskyism became, in Stalinist parlance, a 'tool of foreign powers and of world capitalism.'

One of the major accusations against Trotsky and alleged Trotskyists during the Moscow Trials of 1936-1938 was that they were agents of foreign capital and foreign powers, including intelligence agencies, and were engaged in sabotage against the Soviet State. In particular, with the advent of Nazi Germany in 1933, Stalin sought to show that in the event of war, which he regarded as inevitable, the Trotskyist network in the USSR would serve as a fifth column for Germany.

What is significant is that Khrushchev did concede that Stalin was correct in his fundamental allegation that the Trotskyists, Bukharinites et al represented a faction that sought the 'restoration of capitalism and capitulation to the world bourgeoisie'. However Khrushchev and even Stalin could not go far enough in their denunciation of Trotskyists et al as seeking to 'restore capitalism' and as being agents of foreign powers. To expose the full facts in regard to such accusations would also mean

91

to expose some unpalatable, hidden factors of the Bolshevik Revolution itself, and of Lenin; which would undermine the whole edifice upon which Soviet authority rested – the October 1917 Revolution. Lenin, and Trotsky in particular, had intricate associations with many un-proletarian individuals and interests.

The fact of behind the scenes machinations between the Bolsheviks and international finance was commented upon publicly by two very well-positioned but quite different sources: Henry Wickham Steed, conservative editor of *The London Times*, and Samuel Gompers, head of the American Federation of Labour.

In a first-hand account of the Peace Conference of 1919 Wickham Steed stated that proceedings were interrupted by the return from Moscow of William C Bullitt and Lincoln Steffens, 'who had been sent to Russia towards the middle of February by Colonel House[1] and Mr. Lansing, for the purpose of studying conditions, political and economic, therein for the benefit of the American Commissioners plenipotentiary to negotiate peace.'[2] Steed stated specifically and at some length that international finance was behind the move for recognition of the Bolshevik regime and other moves in favour of the Bolsheviks, stating that: 'Potent international financial interests were at work in favour of the immediate recognition of the Bolshevists.'[3] In return for diplomatic recognition Tchitcherin, the Bolshevist Commissary for Foreign Affairs, was offering 'extensive commercial and economic concessions.'[4]

For his part, Samuel Gompers, the American labour leader, was vehemently opposed to the Bolsheviks and any recognition or commercial transactions, stating to the press in regard to negotiations at the international economic conference at Genoa, that a group of 'predatory international financiers' were working

---

1   American President Woodrow Wilson's principal adviser and confidante.
2   *Henry Wickham Steed, Through Thirty Years 1892-1922* A personal narrative, 'The Peace Conference, The Bullitt Mission', Vol. II. (New York: Doubleday Page and Co., 1924), 301.
3   *Ibid.*
4   *Ibid.*

for the recognition of the Bolshevik regime for the opening up of resources for exploitation. Gompers described this as an 'Anglo-American-German banking group'. He also commented that prominent Americans who had a history of anti-labour attitudes were advocating recognition of the Bolshevik regime.[5]

Trotsky's Banking Connections

What is of significance here however is that Trotsky in particular was the focus of attention by many individuals acting on behalf not only of foreign powers but of international financial institutions. Hence while Stalin and even Khrushchev could aver to the association of Trotsky with foreign powers and even – albeit vaguely – with seeking the 'restoration of capitalism and capitulation to the world bourgeoisie', to trace the links more specifically to international finance would inevitably lead to the association also of the Bolshevik regime per se to those same sources, thus undermining the founding myth of the USSR as being the 'dictatorship of the proletariat'.

These associations between Trotsky and international finance, as well as foreign intelligence services, have been meticulously documented by Dr Richard Spence.[6] Spence states that 'Trotsky was the recipient of mysterious financial assistance and was a person of keen interest to German, Russian and British agents'. Such contentions are very similar to the charges against Trotsky et al at the Moscow Trials, and there are details and personalities involved, said to have been extracted under torture and threats, that are in fact confirmed by Spence, who traces Trotsky's patronage as far back as 1916 when he was an exile from Czarist Russia and was being expelled from a succession of countries in Europe before finding his way to the USA, prior to his return to Russia in 1917 to play his part in the Revolution. Expelled

---

5   Samuel Gompers, 'Soviet Bribe Fund Here Says Gompers, Has Proof That Offers Have Been Made, He Declares, Opposing Recognition. Propaganda Drive. Charges Strong Group of Bankers With Readiness to Accept Lenin's Betrayal of Russia', *The New York Times*, 1 May 1922.

6   Richard B Spence, 'Hidden Agendas: Spies, Lies and Intrigue Surrounding Trotsky's American Visit, January-April 1917', *Revolutionary Russia*, Volume 21, Issue 1 June 2008, 33 – 55.

from France to Spain, Trotsky was locked up as a 'terrorist agitator' for three and a half days in comfortable conditions.[7] Ernst Bark, perhaps with the use of German funds, arranged Trotsky's release and his transfer to Cadiz to await passage with his family to New York and paid for first class passage on the SS Montserrat. Bark was cousin of the Czar's minister of finance Petr Bark who, despite his service to the Czar, had the pro-German, pro-Bolshevik banker Olof Aschberg, of the Nya Banken, Sweden, as his financial agent for his New York dealings. A report reaching US Military Intelligence in 1918 stated that Trotsky had been 'bought by the Germans', and that he was organising the Bolshevik[8] movement with Parvus.

From being penniless in Spain to his arrival in New York, Trotsky had arrived with $500 which Spence states is today's equivalent to about $10,000, although Trotsky liked to depict himself as continuing in proletarian poverty. Immigration authorities also noted that his place of residence would be the less than proletarian Hotel Astor in Times Square.

In New York the Trotsky's lived in a Bronx apartment with all the mod-cons of the day. He was employed by Novyi Mir, and was hosted by Dr Julius Hammer, a Bolshevik who combined revolution with an opulent lifestyle. Hammer was probably the mysterious 'Dr M' referred to by Trotsky in his memoirs, who provided the Trotskys with sightseeing jaunts in his chauffeured car. [9]

One of the main contacts for Trotsky was a maternal uncle, banker and businessman Abram Zhivotovskii. In 1915 Zhivotovskii was jailed in Russia for trading with Germany. The US State Department described Zhivotovskii as outwardly 'very anti-Bolshevik', but who had laundered money to the Bolsheviks and other socialist organizations. [10] He seems to have played a double role in moneymaking, working as a financial agent for both Germans and Allies. During the war he maintained an office

---

7   *Ibid.*
8   It is more accurate to state that Trotsky managed to straddle both the Bolsheviks and the Mensheviks until the impending success of the Bolshevik Revolution in 1917.
9   *Ibid.*
10 *Ibid.*

in Japan under the management of a nephew Iosif Zhivotovskii, who had served as secretary to Sidney Reilly, the so-called 'British Ace of Spies' who nonetheless also seems to have been a duplicitous character in dealing with Germany. Spence mentions that Reilly, who had a business in the USA, had gone to Japan when Trotsky was in Spain, and arrived back in the USA around the time of Trotsky's arrival, the possibility being that Reilly had acquired funds from Trotsky's uncle to give to his nephew in New York. Another Reilly association with Zhivotovskii was via Alexander Weinstein, who had been Zhivotovskii's agent in London, and had joined Reilly in 1916. He was supposedly a loyal Czarist but was identified by American Military Intelligence as a Bolshevik.[11] Of further interest is that Alexander's brother Gregory was business manager of *Novyi Mir,* the newspaper that employed Trotsky while he was in New York. Reilly and Weinstein were also associated with Benny Sverdlov, a Russian arms broker who was the brother of Yakov Sverdlov, the future Soviet commissar.

These multiple connections between Trotsky and Reilly's associates are significant here in that one of the accusations raised during the Moscow Trials was that the Trotskyists had had dealings with 'British spy' Sidney Reilly.

The dealings of Sir William Wiseman, British Military Intelligence chief in the USA, and his deputy Norman Thwaites, with Reilly and associates were concealed even from other British agencies.[12] Wiseman had kept Trotsky under surveillance in New York. Trotsky secured a visa from the British consulate to proceed to Russia via Nova Scotia and Scandinavia. The Passport Control Section of the British Consulate was under the direction of Thwaites. Trotsky was to remark on his arrival in Russia about the helpful attitude of consular officials, despite his detention as a possible German agent by Canadian authorities at Nova Scotia. Trotsky had been able to pay for tickets aboard the Kristianiafiord for himself and his family, and also for a small

---

11   Military Intelligence Division, 9140-6073, Memorandum # 2, 23 August 1918, 2. Cited
      by Spence, op.cit.
12   Spence, *Ibid.*

entourage. What is additionally interesting about Wiseman is that he was closely associated with banking interests, and around 1921 joined Kuhn, Loeb and Co.[13] In 1955 Wiseman launched his own international bank with investments from Kuhn, Loeb & Co.; Rothschild; Rockefeller; Warburg firms, et al[14]. He was thus very close to the international banking dynasties throughout much of his life.

To return to the Kristianiafiord however, on board with Trotsky and his entourage, first class, were Robert Jivotovsky (Zhivotovskii), likely to have been another Trotsky cousin; Israel Fundaminsky, whom Trotsky regarded as a British agent, and Andrei Kalpaschnikoff, who acted as translator when Trotsky was being questioned by British authorities at Nova Scotia. Kalpaschnikoff was closely associated with Vladimir Rogovine, who worked for Weinstein and Reilly. Kalpaschnikoff was also associated with John MacGregor Grant, a friend and business partner of both Reilly and Olof Aschberg. We can therefore see an intricate connection between British super-spy Reilly, and bankers such as Aschberg, who served as a conduit of funds to the Bolsheviks, and Zhivotovskii via Alexander Weinstein.

When Trotsky and several of his entourage were arrested on 29 March at Nova Scotia and questioned by authorities regarding associations with Germany this could well have been an act to dispel any suspicions that Trotsky might be serving British interests. The British had the option of returning him to New York but allowed him to proceed to Russia. [15]

The attitude of Wiseman towards the Bolsheviks once they had achieved nominal power was one of urging recognition, Wiseman cabling President Wilson's principal adviser Col. Edward House on 1 May 1918 that the allies should intervene at the invitation of the Bolsheviks and help organise the Bolshevik army then fighting the White Armies during the Civil War.[16]

---

13   Wiseman became a partner in 1929.
14   'Sir William's New Bank', *Time*, October 17 1955.
15   The foregoing on Trotsky's associations from Spain to New York and his transit back to Russia are indebted to Spence, op.cit.
16   Edward M. House, ed. Charles Seymour, *The Intimate Papers of Col. House* (New

This would accord with the aim of certain international bankers to secure recognition of the Bolshevik regime, as noted by both Gompers and Steed.

The financial interests in the USA that formed around the Council on Foreign Relations (CFR), founded by presidential adviser Col. Edward M House as a foreign policy think tank of businessmen, politicians and intellectuals, were clamouring for recognition of the Soviets. The CFR issued a report on Bolshevik Russia in 1923, prompted by Lenin's 'New Economic Policy'. The report repudiated anti-Bolshevik attitudes and fears that Bolshevism would be spread to other countries (although it had already had a brief but bloody reign in Hungary and revolts in German). CFR historian Peter Grosse writes that the report stated that,

> the Bolsheviks were on their way to 'sanity and sound business practices,' the Council study group concluded, but the welcome to foreign concessionaires would likely be short-lived.... Thus, the Council experts recommended in March 1923 that American businessmen get into Russia while Lenin's invitation held good...[17]

Armand Hammer, head of Occidental Petroleum, son of the aforementioned Dr Julius Hammer who had been the Trotsky family's host in New York, was a globetrotting plutocrat who mixed with the political and business elites of the world for decades. Hammer was in intimate contact with every Soviet leader from Lenin to Gorbachev — except for Stalin.[18] This omission is indicative of the rift that had occurred between the USSR and Western financial and industrial interests with the assumption of Stalin and the defeat of Trotsky. The CFR report on the USSR that advised American business to get in quick before the situation changed, was prescient. In 1921 Hammer was in the USSR sewing up business deals. Hammer met Trotsky, who

---

York: Houghton, Mifflin Co.), Vol. III, 421.

17 Peter Grosse, Continuing The Inquiry: The Council on Foreign Relations from 1921 to 1996, (New York: Council on Foreign Relations, 2006), 'Basic Assumptions'. The entire book can be read online at: http://www.cfr.org/about/history/cfr/index.html

18 Armand Hammer, *Witness to History* (London: Coronet Books, 1988), 221.

asked him whether 'financial circles in the USA regard Russia as a desirable field of investment?' Trotsky continued:

> Inasmuch as Russia had its Revolution, capital was really safer there than anywhere else because, 'whatever should happen abroad, the Soviet would adhere to any agreements it might make. Suppose one of your Americans invests money in Russia. When the Revolution comes to America, his property will of course be nationalised, but his agreement with us will hold good and he will thus be in a much more favourable position than the rest of his fellow capitalists.'[19]

In contrast to the obliging Trotsky who was willing to guarantee the wealth and investments of Big Business, Hammer said of Stalin:

> I never met Stalin and I never had any dealing with him. However it was perfectly clear to me in 1930 that Stalin was not a man with whom you could do business. Stalin believed that the state was capable of running everything, without the support of foreign concessionaires and private enterprise. That was the main reason why I left Moscow: I could see that I would soon be unable to do business there...[20]

As for Trotsky's attitude toward capitalist investment, were the charges brought against Trotsky et al during the Moscow Trials wholly cynical efforts to disparage and eliminate the perceived opposition to Stalin's authority, or was there at least some factual basis to the charge that the Trotskyist-Left and Bukharin-Right blocs sought to 'restore capitalism' to the USSR? It is of interest in this respect to note that even according to one of Trotsky's present-day exponents, David North, Trotsky 'placed greater emphasis than any other Soviet leader of his time on the overriding importance of close economic links between the USSR and the world capitalist market'. North speaking to an Australian

---

19   *Ibid.*, 160.
20   *Ibid.*, 221.

Trotskyist conference went on to state of Trotsky's attitude:

> Soviet economic development, he insisted, required both access to the resources of the world market and the intelligent utilisation of the international division of labour. The development of economic planning required at minimum a knowledge of competitive advantage and efficiencies at the international level. It served no rational economic purpose for the USSR to make a virtue of frittering away its own limited resources in a vain effort to duplicate on Soviet soil what it could obtain at far less cost on the world capitalist market.... It is helpful to keep in mind that Trotsky belonged to a generation of Russian Marxists who had utilised the opportunity provided by revolutionary exile to carefully observe and study the workings of the capitalist system in the advanced countries. They were familiar not only with the oft-described 'horrors' of capitalism, but also with its positive achievements. ... Trotsky argued that a vital precondition for the development of the Soviet economy along socialist lines was its assimilation of the basic techniques of capitalist management, organisation, accounting and production.[21]

It was against this background that during the latter half of the 1930s Stalin acted against the Trotsky and Bukharin blocs as agents of world capitalism and foreign powers. The most cogent defence of the Moscow Trials, *The Great Conspiracy Against Russia*,[22] was written by two American journalists, Albert E Kahn and Michael Sayers, and carried an endorsement by former US ambassador to the USSR, Joseph Davis, who had witnessed the trials.

---

21   David North, 'Leon Trotsky and the Fate of Socialism in the 20th Century', opening lecture to the International Summer School on 'Marxism and the Fundamental Problems of the 20th Century', organised by the International Committee of the Fourth International and the Socialist Equality Party of Australia, Sydney, Australia, January 3 1998. David North is the national secretary of the Socialist Equality Party in the USA, and has lectured extensively in Europe, Asia, the US and Russia on Marxism and the program of the Fourth International. http://www.wsws.org/exhibits/trotsky/trlect. htm (accessed 12 March 2010).

22   Albert E Kahn and Michael Sayers, *The Great Conspiracy Against Russia*, (London: Collet's Holdings Ltd., 1946).

Among the charges against Trotsky was that he was in contact with British Intelligence operatives, and was conspiring against Lenin. This is not altogether implausible. Lenin and the Bolshevik faction were in favour of a separate peace between Russia and Germany. Lenin and his entourage had been provided with funds and transport by the German General Staff to travel back to Russia,[23] while Trotsky's return from New York to Russia had been facilitated by British and American Intelligence interests. Kahn and Sayers commented that 'for fourteen years, Trotsky had fiercely opposed the Bolsheviks; then in August 1917, a few months before the Bolshevik Revolution he had joined Lenin's party and risen to power with it. Within the Bolshevik Party, Trotsky was organizing a Left Opposition to Lenin.'[24]

Trotsky was not well disposed to negotiate peace with German imperialists, and it was a major point of debate among the Allies whether certain socialist revolutionaries could be won over to the Allied cause. Trotsky himself had stated in the offices of *Novy Mir* just before his departure from New York to Russia that although revolutionists would soon overthrow the Kerensky regime they 'would not make a separate peace with Germany'.[25] From this perspective it would have made sense for William Wiseman to have intervened and for the British authorities to have let Trotsky proceed after having detained him at Nova Scotia.

American mining magnate and banker Colonel William Boyce Thompson, head of the American Red Cross Mission in Russia,[26] was eager to recruit the Bolsheviks for the Allied cause. He stated his intention of providing $1,000,000 of his own money to assist with Bolshevik propaganda directed at Germany and

---

23   Antony Sutton, op.cit., 39-42.

24   Kahn and Sayers, op.cit. 29.

25   'Calls People War Weary, But Leo Trotsky Says They Do Tot Want Separate Peace', *The New York Times*, 16 March 1917.

26   The real purpose of the American Red Cross Mission in Russia was to examine how commercial relations could be established with the fledgling Bolshevik regime, as indicated by the fact that there were more business representatives in the Mission than there were medical personnel. See: Dr Anton Sutton, *Wall Street and the Bolshevik Revolution* (New York: Arlington House Publishers, 1974), 71-88. K R Bolton, *Revolution from Above* (London: Arktos Media Ltd., 2011) 63-64.

Austria. [27] Thompson's insistence that if the Allies recognised the Bolsheviks they would not make a separate peace with Germany,[28] accorded with Trotsky's own attitude insofar as he also wished to see the war end not with a separate peace but with revolutions that would bring down Germany and Austria. His agenda therefore seems to have been quite distinct from that of Lenin's, and might point to separate sources of funds that were provided to them.

Trotsky's actions when the Bolsheviks assumed power were consistent with his declarations, and went against Lenin's policy of ending the war with Germany. As Foreign Commissar Trotsky had been sent to Brest-Litovsk 'with categorical instructions from Lenin to sign peace.'[29] Instead he called for a Communist uprising in Germany, and stated that although the Russian army could no longer continue in the war and would demobilise, the Soviets would not sign a peace agreement. After Trotsky's rhetoric at Brest-Litovsk the Germans launched another assault on the Eastern Front, and the new Red Army found itself still fighting the Germans.

It was at this point that R H Bruce Lockhart, special agent of the British War Cabinet, sought out Trotsky, on the instructions from British Prime Minister Lloyd George.

Lockhart, generally considered the typical anti-Bolshevik Establishment figure, was actually well disposed towards the Bolsheviks and like Colonel Thompson, hoped to win them over to the Allies. At one point his wife warned that his colleagues in Britain thought he might be going 'Red'. Lockhart wrote of the situation:

> Russia was out of the war. Bolshevism would last - certainly as long as the war lasted. I deprecated as sheer folly our militarist propaganda, because it took no account

27 'Gives Bolsheviki a Million', *Washington Post*, 2 February 1918, cited by Sutton, op.cit., ., 82-83.
28 *The New York Times*, 27 January 1918, op.cit.
29 Kahn and Sayers, op.cit., 29.

of the war-weariness which had raised the Bolsheviks to the supreme power. In my opinion, we had to take the Bolshevik peace proposals seriously. Our policy should now aim at achieving an anti-German peace in Russia'.[30]

Coincidentally, 'an anti-German peace in Russia' seems to precisely describe the aim of Trotsky.

Trotsky intended that the World War would be transformed into a revolutionary war, with the starting point being revolutions in Germany and Austria. This would certainly accord with Colonel Thompson's intentions to fund Bolshevist propaganda in Germany and Austria with $1,000,000. Thompson was in communication with Trotsky via Raymond Robins, his deputy with the Red Cross Mission, and like him an enthusiast for the Bolshevik regime.[31] Lloyd George had met Thompson and had been won over to the aim of contacting Lenin and Trotsky. Lockhart was instructed to return to Russia to establish 'unofficial contact with the Bolsheviks'.[32] Lockhart relates that he met Trotsky for two hours at the latter's office at Smolny. While Lockhart was highly impressed with Trotsky he did not regard the Foreign Commissar as able to wield sufficient influence to replace Lenin. Trotsky's parting words to Lockhart at this first meeting were: 'Now is the big opportunity for the Allied Governments'. Thereafter Lockhart saw Trotsky on a daily basis. [33] Lockhart stated that Trotsky was willing to bring Soviet Russia over to Britain:

He considered that war was inevitable. If the Allies would send a promise of support, he informed me that he would sway the decision of the Government in favour of war. I sent several telegrams to London requesting an official message that would enable me to strengthen Trotsky's hands. No message was sent.[34]

30   *R H Bruce Lockhart, British Agent* (London: G P Putnam's Sons, 1933), Book Four, 'History From the Inside', Chapter I.

31   Antony Sutton, op.cit., 84, 86.

32   R H Bruce Lockhart, op.cit.

33   *Ibid.*, Chapter III.

34   *Ibid.*

Given Trotsky's position in regard to Germany, and the statements of Lockhart in his memoirs, the Stalinist accusation is entirely plausible that Trotsky was the focus of Allied support, and would explain why the British expedited Trotsky's return to Russia. Indeed, Lockhart was to remark that the British view was that they might be able to make use of the dissensions between Trotsky and Lenin, and believed that the Allies could reach an accord with Soviet Russia because of the extravagant peace demands of the Germans.[35] However from what Lockhart sates, it seems that the Allied procrastination in regard to recognition of the Bolsheviks was the uncertainty that they constituted a stable and lasting Government, and that they were suspicious of the Bolshevik intentions towards Germany, with Lenin and Trotsky still widely regarded as German agents. [36]

The period preceding World War II, particularly the signing of the Anti-Comintern Pact between Germany, Italy and Japan, served as a catalyst for Stalin's offensive against Trotskyists and other suspect elements. Trotsky had since his exile been promoted in the West as the great leader of the Bolshevik Revolution[37], while his own background had been one of opportunism, for the most part as an anti-Leninist Menshevik. [38] It was only in August 1917, seeing the situation in Russia, that Trotsky applied for membership of the Bolshevik Party.[39] Trotsky had joined the Bolshevik Party with his entire faction, a faction that remained intact within the Soviet apparatus, and was ready to be activated after Stalin's election as General Secretary in 1922. Trotsky admits to a revolutionary network from 1923 when he wrote in his 1938 eulogy to his son Leon Sedov: 'Leon threw himself headlong into the work of the Opposition...Thus, at seventeen, he began the life of a fully conscious revolutionist, quickly

---

35   *Ibid.* Lockhart observed that while the German peace terms received 112 votes from the Central Executive Committee of the Bolshevik Party, there had been 86 against, and 25 abstentions, among the latter of whom was Trotsky.

36   *Ibid.,* Chapter IV.

37   That at least was the perception of Stalinists of Trotsky's depiction by the West, as portrayed by Kahn and Sayers, op.cit., 194.

38   Kahn and Sayers cite a number of Lenin's statements regarding Trotsky, dating from 1911, when Lenin stated that Trotsky slides from one faction to another and back again, but ultimately 'I must declare that Trotsky represents his own faction only...' *Ibid.,* 195.

39   *Ibid.,* 199.

grasped the art of conspiratorial work, illegal meetings, and the secret issuing and distribution of Opposition documents. The Komsomol (Communist Youth organization) rapidly developed its own cadres of Opposition leaders.'[40] Hence Trotsky had freely admitted to the fundamental charges of the Stalinist regime: the existence of a widespread Trotskyist 'conspiracy'. Indeed, as far back as 1921, the Central Committee of the Bolshevik Party had already passed a resolution banning all 'factions' in the Party, specifically warning Trotsky against 'factional activities', and condemning the factionalist activities of what the resolution called 'Trotskyites'. [41]

In 1924 Trotsky met with Boris Savinkov, a Socialist Revolutionary, who had served as head of the terrorist wing, the so-called 'Fighting Organization', of the Party, and who had been Deputy Minister of War in the Kerensky Government. After the triumph of the Bolsheviks Savinkov, leaving Russia in 1920, became associated with French and Polish authorities, and with British agents Lockhart[42] and Sidney Reilly. [43] Savinkov was involved in counter-revolutionary activities, in trying to form an army to overthrow the Bolsheviks. Winston Churchill confirms Savinkov's meeting with Trotsky in 1924, Churchill himself being involved in the anti-Soviet machinations, writing in his *Great Contemporaries:* 'In June 1924, Kamenev and Trotsky definitely invited him (Savinkov) to return'.[44]

In 1924 a leading Trotskyite, Christian Rakovsky, arrived in Britain as Soviet Ambassador. According to the testimony at the Moscow Trial during March 1938 Rakovsky admitted to meeting two British agents, Lockhart and Captain Armstrong.

---

40   Leon Trotsky, *Leon Sedov: Son-Friend-Fighter,* 1938, cited by Kahn and Sayers, 205.
41   *Ibid.,* 204.
42   R H Bruce Lockhart, op.cit., Book Three: War & Peace, Chapter IX. Lockhart described Savinkov as a professional 'schemer', who 'had mingled so much with spies and agents-provocateurs that, like the hero in his own novel, he hardly knew whether he was deceiving himself or those whom he meant to deceive'. Lockhart commented that Savinkov had 'entirely captivated Mr Churchill, who saw in him a Russian Bonaparte'.
43   Reilly, the British 'super agent' although widely known for his anti-Bolshevik views, prior to his becoming a 'super spy' and possibly working for the intelligence agencies of four states, by his own account had been arrested in 1892 in Russia by the Czarist secret police as a messenger for the revolutionary Friends of Enlightenment.
44   Kahn and Sayers, op.cit., 208.

Rakovsky is said to have confessed at this trial that Lockhart and Armstrong had told him that he had been permitted entry into Britain because of his association with Trotsky, as they wanted to cultivate relations with the latter. When Rakovsky reported back to Trotsky several months later, Trotsky was alleged to have been interested.

In 1926 Rakovsky was transferred to France prior to which he was alleged to have been instructed by Trotsky to seek out contacts with 'conservatives circles' who might support an uprising, as Trotsky considered the situation in Russia to be right for a coup. Rakovsky, as instructed, met several French industrialists, including the grain merchant Louis Dreyfus, and the flax merchant Nicole, both Deputies of the French Parliament.[45] Rakovsky in his testimony during the 1936 trial of Bukharin, et al, Rakovsky being one of the defendants, relates the manner by which he was approached by various intelligence agencies, including those of Japan when in 1934 Rakovsky was head of a Soviet Red Cross Delegation.[46] Rakovsky spoke of the difficulty the Trotskyites had in maintaining relations with both British and Japanese intelligence agencies, since the two states were becoming antagonistic over problems in China.[47] Rakovsky explained that: 'We Trotskyites have to play three cards at the present moment: the German, Japanese and British'[48] At that time the Trotskyites – or at least Rakovsky - regarded the likelihood of a Japanese attack on the USSR as more likely than a German attack. Rakovsky even then alluded to his belief that an accord between Hitler and Stalin was possible. It seems plausible enough that Trotskyites were indeed looking toward an invasion of the USSR as the means of destabilising the regime during which Trotskyist cells could launch their counter-revolution. Certainly we know from the account of Churchill that Trotsky met the ultra-terrorist Socialist Revolutionary Savinkov, who was himself involved with British Intelligence via Reilly

---

45   Commissariat of Justice, Report of the Case of the Anti-Soviet 'Bloc of Rights and Trotskyites', Heard Before The Military Collegium of the Court of the USSR, Moscow, March 24 1938, 307.

46   *Ibid.,* 288.

47   *Ibid.* 293.

48   *Ibid.*

and Lockhart. Rakovsky stated of a possible Hitler-Stalin Pact:

> Personally I thought that the possibility was not excluded that Hitler would seek a rapprochement with the government of the USSR. I cited the policy of Richelieu: in his own country he exterminated the Protestants, while in his foreign policy he concluded alliances with the Protestant German princes. The relations between Germany and Poland were still in the stage of their inception at the time. Japan, on the other hand, was a potent aggressor against the USSR. For us Trotskyites the Japanese card was extremely important, but, on the other hand, we should not overrate the importance of Japan as our ally against the Soviet government.[49]

As far as the Stalinist allegations go in regard to the Trotskyists aligning with foreign powers and viewing an invasion of the USSR as a catalyst for revolution, other ultra-Marxists had taken paths far more unlikely. As mentioned Savinkov, who had been one of the most violent of the Socialist Revolutionaries in Czarist Russia, had sought out British assistance in forming a counter-revolutionary army. Savinkov had fled to Poland in 1919 where he tried to organize 'the evacuation committee' within the Polish armies then attacking Russia.[50] Savinkov's colleagues in Poland, Merezhkovsky, and his wife Zinaida Hippius, who had been ardent Socialist Revolutionary propagandists, later became supporters of Mussolini and then of Hitler, in the hope of overthrowing Stalin[51]. Therefore the Stalinist allegation of Trotskyite collusion even with Fascist powers is plausible.

It is the same road that resulted in the alliance of many Trotskyists, Mensheviks and other Leftists with the CIA, and their metamorphoses into ardent Cold Warriors. It is the same road that brought leading American Trotsky apologist Professor Sidney

---

49   *Ibid.*
50   Bernice Glatzer Rosenthal, 'Eschatology and the Appeal of Revolution', *California Slavic Studies,* Volume. II, University of California Press, California, 1930, 116.
51   *Ibid.*

Hook, 'a lifelong Menshevik', to the leadership of a major CIA front, the previously considered Congress for Cultural Freedom.

Max Shachtman

Max Shachtman, one of Trotsky's leading representatives in the USA[52], is pivotal when considering why Trotskyites became ardent Cold Warriors, CIA front men, apologists for US foreign policy, and continue to champion the USA as the only 'truly revolutionary' state.

Expelled from the Communist Party USA in 1928 Shachtman co-founded the Communist League and the Socialist Workers Party. He then split to form the Workers Party of the United States in 1940, which became the Independent Socialist League and merged with the Socialist Party in 1958.[53] The Socialist Party factionalised into the Democratic Socialists and the Social Democrats.

Shachtman was of course scathing of the Moscow Trials. His critique is standard, and will not be of concern here.[54] What is of interest is Shachtman's surpassing of Trotsky himself in his opposition to the USSR, his faction (the so-called 'Third Camp') being what he considered as a purified, genuine Trotskyism, which eventuated into apologists for US foreign policy.

The Shachtmanist critique of the USSR was that it had at an early stage been transformed from 'government 'bureaucratism to 'party bureaucratism'.[55] 'Soviet bureaucratism became party bureaucratism. In increasing numbers the government official was the party official.'[56] 'We do not have a workers' state but a workers' state with bureaucratic deformations', Shachtman

---

52 Shachtman was one of the two most prominent Trotskyites in the USA according to Trotskyist historian Ernest Haberkern, Introduction to Max Shachtman, http://www.marxists.org/archive/shachtma/intro.htm

53 'British Trotskyism in 1931', Encyclopaedia of Trotskyism Online: Revolutionary History, http://www.marxists.org/history/etol/revhist/backiss/vol1/no1/glotzer.html

54 Max Shachtman, *Behind the Moscow Trial* (New York: Pioneer Publishers, 1936).

55 Max Shachtman, 'Trotsky Begins the Fight', *The Struggle for the New Course* (New York: New International Publishing Co., 1943).

56 *Ibid.*

stated in quoting Trotsky as far back as 1922. And again from Trotsky: 'We have a bureaucracy not only in the Soviet institutions, but in the institutions of the party'... Shachtman continues: 'A month later, in a veiled public attack upon Stalin as head of the Workers' and Peasants' Inspection, he repeated his view that the state machine was still "a survival to a large extent of the former bureaucracy ... with only a superficial new coat of paint."[57]

While in 1937 Shachtman declared that the USSR should nonetheless be defended against aggression from, for example, Nazi Germany and that it was a Stalinist slur to think that Trotsky would be an enemy of the USSR in such circumstances[58], by 1940 Shachtman was at loggerheads with Trotsky himself and the 'Cannon'[59] group in the Workers Party.

The Trotskyites were agreed that Stalinist Russia had become a 'degenerated' workers' state,' however the Cannon-Trotsky line and the position of the Fourth International was that should the USSR be attacked by capitalist or fascist powers, because it still had a so-called 'progressive' economy based on the nationalisation of property, the USSR must be defended on that basis alone. The Shachtman line, on the other hand, argued from what they considered to be a dialectical position:

> Just as it was once necessary, in connection with the trade union problem, to speak concretely of what kind of workers' state exists in the Soviet Union, so it is necessary to establish, in connection with the present war, the degree of the degeneration of the Soviet state. The dialectical method of treating such questions makes this mandatory upon us. And the degree of the degeneration of the regime cannot be established by abstract reference to the existence of nationalized property, but only by observing the realities of living events.

---

57   *Ibid.*
58   Leon Trotsky, *In Defence of the Soviet Union*, Max Shachtman, 'Introduction.' (New York: Pioneer Publishers, 1937).
59   James P Cannon, a veteran Trotskyist and former colleague of Shachtman's.

The Fourth International established, years ago, the fact that the Stalinist regime (even though based upon nationalized property) had degenerated to the point where it was not only capable of conducting reactionary wars against the proletariat and its revolutionary vanguard, and even against colonial peoples, but did in fact conduct such wars. Now, in our opinion, on the basis of the actual course of Stalinist policy (again, even though based upon nationalized property), the Fourth International must establish the fact that the Soviet Union (i.e., the ruling bureaucracy and the armed forces serving it) has degenerated to the point where it is capable of conducting reactionary wars even against capitalist states (Poland, Estonia, Lithuania, Latvia, now Finland, and tomorrow Rumania and elsewhere). This is the point which forms the nub of our difference with you and with the Cannon faction.[60]

Shachtman now expressed his approach unequivocally:

War is a continuation of politics, and if Stalinist policy, even in the occupied territory where property has been statified, preserves completely its reactionary character, then the war it is conducting is reactionary. In that case, the revolutionary proletariat must refuse to give the Kremlin and its army material and military aid. It must concentrate all efforts on overturning the Stalinist regime. That is not our war! Our war is against the counterrevolutionary bureaucracy at the present time!

In other words, I propose, in the present war, a policy of revolutionary defeatism in the Soviet Union, as explained in the statement of the Minority on the Russian question – and in making this proposal I do not feel myself one whit less a revolutionary class patriot than I have always been.[61]

That was the Shachtmanite line during World War II: that it

---

60   Max Shachtman, 'The Crisis in the American Party: An Open Letter in Reply to Comrade Leon Trotsky', *New International*, Vol.6 No.2, March 1940), 43-51.
61   *Ibid.*

was better that Nazi Germany defeated Stalin than that the 'degenerated workers' state' should continue to exist. The same thinking emerged during the Cold War, shortly after World War II, when Shachtman began to speak about the threat of Stalinist parties throughout the world as agencies for Soviet policy, a theme that would become a basis of US attitudes towards the USSR:

> The Stalinist parties are indeed agents of the Kremlin oligarchy, no matter what country they function in. The interests and the fate of these Stalinist parties are inseparably intertwined with the interests and fate of the Russian bureaucracy. The Stalinist parties are everywhere based upon the power of the Russian bureaucracy, they serve this power, they are dependent upon it, and they cannot live without it.[62]

By 1948 Shachtmanism as a Cold Warrior apologia for American foreign policy was taking shape. In seeing positive signs in the Titoist Yugoslavia break with the USSR, Shachtman wrote:

> In the first place, the division in the capitalist camp is, to all practical intents, at an end. In any case, there is nothing like the division that existed from 1939 onward and which gave Stalinist Russia such tremendous room for maneuvering. In spite of all the differences that still exist among them, the capitalist world under American imperialist leadership and drive is developing an increasingly solid front against Russian imperialism.[63]

In other words, Shachtman saw unity among the capitalist states against Stalinist Russia as a positive sign. The overthrow of Stalinism became the first priority of Shachtmanite Trotskyism in the Cold War era, as it had during World War II.

In 1948 Shachtman scathingly attacked the position of the

---

62 Max Shachtman, 'The Nature of the Stalinist Parties: Their Class Roots, Political Role and Basic Aim', The *New International: A Monthly Organ of Revolutionary Marxism*, Vol.13 No.3, March 1947, 69-74.

63 Max Shachtman, 'Stalinism on the Decline: Tito versus Stalin The Beginning of the End of the Russian Empire', *New International*, Vol. XIV No.6, August 1948, 172-178.

Fourth International in having continued to defend the USSR as a 'degenerated workers' state', and of its mistaken belief that the Stalinist 'bureaucratic dictatorship' would fall apart during World War II. He pointed out that Stalinist imperialism had emerged from the war victorious.[64] From here it was but a short way for the Shachtmanites to embrace the Cold War opposition to the USSR, and for the heirs of this to continue as enthusiasts for US foreign policy to the present-day.

By 1950 Stalinism had become the major problem for world socialism, Shachtman now writing as head of the Independent Socialist League:

> The principal new problem faced by Marxian theory, and therewith Marxian practice, is the problem of Stalinism. What once appeared to many to be either an academic or 'foreign' problem is now, it should at last be obvious, a decisive problem for all classes in all countries. If it is understood as a purely Russian phenomenon or as a problem 'in itself,' it is of course not understood at all.[65]

Natalia Sedova Trotsky

Natalia Sedova, Trotsky's widow, endorsed the Shachtmanite line, declaring that the American-led alliance against the USSR would have been approved by her late husband. Her letter of resignation to the Fourth International and to the Socialist Workers Party (USA) is worth reproducing in its entirety:

> You know quite well that I have not been in political agreement with you for the past five or six years, since the end of the [Second World] war and even earlier. The position you have taken on the important events of recent

---

64 Max Shachtman, 'The Congress of the Fourth International: An Analysis of the Bankruptcy of "Orthodox Trotskyism"', *New International*, Vol.XIV, No.8, October 1948, 236-245.

65 Max Shachtman, 'Reflections on a Decade Past: On the Tenth Anniversary of Our Movement', *The New International: A Monthly Organ of Revolutionary Marxism*, Vol.16 No.3, May-June 1950, 131-144.

times shows me that, instead of correcting your earlier errors, you are persisting in them and deepening them. On the road you have taken, you have reached a point where it is no longer possible for me to remain silent or to confine myself to private protests. I must now express my opinions publicly.

The step which I feel obliged to take has been a grave and difficult one for me, and I can only regret it sincerely. But there is no other way. After a great deal of reflections and hesitations over a problem which pained me deeply, I find that I must tell you that I see no other way than to say openly that our disagreements make it impossible for me to remain any longer in your ranks.

The reasons for this final action on my part are known to most of you. I repeat them here briefly only for those to whom they are not familiar, touching only on our fundamentally important differences and not on the differences over matters of daily policy which are related to them or which follow from them.

Obsessed by old and outlived formulas, you continue to regard the Stalinist state as a workers' state. I cannot and will not follow you in this.

Virtually every year after the beginning of the fight against the usurping Stalinist bureaucracy, L D Trotsky repeated that the regime was moving to the right, under conditions of a lagging world revolution and the seizure of all political positions in Russia by the bureaucracy. Time and again, he pointed out how the consolidation of Stalinism in Russia led to the worsening of the economic, political and social positions of the working class, and the triumph of a tyrannical and privileged aristocracy. If this trend continues, he said, the revolution will be at an end and the restoration of capitalism will be achieved.

That, unfortunately, is what has happened even if in new and unexpected forms. There is hardly a country in the world where the authentic ideas and bearers of socialism are so barbarously hounded. It should be clear to everyone that the revolution has been completely destroyed by Stalinism. Yet you continue to say that under this unspeakable regime, Russia is still a workers' state. I consider this a blow at socialism. Stalinism and the Stalinist state have nothing whatever in common with a workers' state or with socialism. They are the worst and the most dangerous enemies of socialism and the working class.

You now hold that the states of Eastern Europe over which Stalinism established its domination during and after the war, are likewise workers' states. This is equivalent to saying that Stalinism has carried out a revolutionary socialist role. I cannot and will not follow you in this.

After the war and even before it ended, there was a rising revolutionary movement of the masses in these Eastern countries. But it was not these masses that won power and it was not a workers' state that was established by their struggle. It was the Stalinist counterrevolution that won power, reducing these lands to vassals of the Kremlin by strangling the working masses, their revolutionary struggles and their revolutionary aspirations.

By considering that the Stalinist bureaucracy established workers' states in these countries, you assign to it a progressive and even revolutionary role. By propagating this monstrous falsehood to the workers' vanguard, you deny to the Fourth International all the basic reasons for existence as the world party of the socialist revolution. In the past, we always considered Stalinism to be a counterrevolutionary force in every sense of the term. You no longer do so. But I continue to do so.

In 1932 and 1933, the Stalinists, in order to justify their shameless capitulation to Hitlerism, declared that it would matter little if the Fascists came to power because socialism would come after and through the rule of Fascism. Only dehumanized brutes without a shred of socialist thought or spirit could have argued this way. Now, notwithstanding the revolutionary aims which animate you, you maintain that the despotic Stalinist reaction which has triumphed in Europe is one of the roads through which socialism will eventually come. This view marks an irredeemable break with the profoundest convictions always held by our movement and which I continue to share.

I find it impossible to follow you in the question of the Tito regime in Yugoslavia. All the sympathy and support of revolutionists and even of all democrats, should go to the Yugoslav people in their determined resistance to the efforts of Moscow to reduce them and their country to vassalage. Every advantage should be taken of the concessions which the Yugoslav regime now finds itself obliged to make to the people. But your entire press is now devoted to an inexcusable idealization of the Titoist bureaucracy for which no ground exists in the traditions and principles of our movement.

This bureaucracy is only a replica, in a new form, of the old Stalinist bureaucracy. It was trained in the ideas, the politics and morals of the GPU. Its regime differs from Stalin's in no fundamental regard. It is absurd to believe or to teach that the revolutionary leadership of the Yugoslav people will develop out of this bureaucracy or in any way other than in the course of struggle against it.

Most insupportable of all is the position on the war to which you have committed yourselves. The third world war which threatens humanity confronts the revolutionary movement with the most difficult problems, the most complex situations, the gravest decisions. Our position can be taken only after the most earnest and freest discussions. But in the face of all the events of recent years, you continue to advocate, and to pledge the entire movement to, the defense of the Stalinist state. You are even now supporting the armies of Stalinism in the war which is being endured by the anguished Korean people. I cannot and will not follow you in this.

As far back as 1927, Trotsky, in reply to a disloyal question put to him in the Political Bureau [of the Soviet Communist Party] by Stalin, stated his views as follows: For the socialist fatherland, yes! For the Stalinist regime, no! That was in 1927! Now, twenty-three years later Stalin has left nothing of the socialist fatherland. It has been replaced by the enslavement and degradation of the people by the Stalinist autocracy. This is the state you propose to defend in the war, which you are already defending in Korea.

I know very well how often you repeat that you are criticizing Stalinism and fighting it. But the fact is that your criticism and your fight lose their value and can yield no results because they are determined by and subordinated to your position of defense of the Stalinist state. Whoever defends this regime of barbarous oppression, regardless of the motives, abandons the principles of socialism and internationalism.

In the message sent me from the recent convention of the SWP you write that Trotsky's ideas continue to be your guide. I must tell you that I read these words with great bitterness. As you observe from what I have written above, I do not see his ideas in your politics. I have confidence in these ideas. I remain convinced that the only way out of the present situation is the social revolution, the self-emancipation of the proletariat of the world.[66]

Natalia Trotsky, like the Shachtmanites, regarded the USSR as having irredeemably destroyed Marxism, and that the only option left was to destroy the USSR, which meant aligning with the USA in the Cold War.

---

66   Natalia Sedova Trotsky, May 9, 1951, *Labor Action,* June 17, 1951, http://www.marxists. org/history/etol/newspape/socialistvoice/natalia38.html

It was this bellicose anti-Stalinism that brought the Shachtmanites into the US foreign policy establishment during the Cold War, and beyond, to the present-day. Haberkern, an admirer of Shachtman's early commitment to Trotskyism and opposition to Stalinism, lamented:

> There is, unfortunately, a sad footnote to Shachtman's career. Beginning in the 50s he began to move to the right in response to the discouraging climate of the Cold War. He ended up a Cold Warrior and apologist for the Meany wing of the AFL-CIO.[67] But that should not diminish the value of his earlier contributions.[68]

Cold War and Beyond

Professor Hook and Max Shachtman veered increasingly towards a pro-US position to the point that Hook, while maintaining his commitment to Social-Democracy, voted for Richard Nixon and publicly defended President Ronald Reagan's policies.

During the 1960s, Hook critiqued the New Left and became an outspoken supporter of the Vietnam War. In 1984 he was selected by the National Endowment for the Humanities to give the annual Jefferson Lecture, 'the highest honor the federal government confers for distinguished intellectual achievement in the humanities'. [69] On 23 May 1985 Hook was awarded the Presidential Medal of Freedom by President Reagan for being one of the first 'to warn the intellectual world of its moral obligations and personal stake in the struggle between freedom and totalitarianism.[70] Edward S Shapiro writing in the American 'conservative' journal First Principles, summarised Hook's position:

---

67 American Federation of Labor-Central Industrial Organization.
68 Haberkern, op.cit.
69 Sidney Hook, 'Education in Defense of a Free Society', 1984, Jefferson Lecture in the Humanities, National Endowment for Humanities, http://www.neh.gov/whoweare/jefflect.html
70 Edward S Shapiro, 'Hook Sidney', First Principles: The Home of American Intellectual Conservatism, 3 July 2009.

One of America's leading anti-communist intellectuals,[71] Hook supported American entry into the Korean War, the isolation of Red China, the efforts of the United States government to maintain a qualitative edge in nuclear weapons, the Johnson administration's attempt to preserve a pro-western regime in South Vietnam, and the campaign of the Reagan administration to overthrow the communist regime in Nicaragua.

Those both within and outside of conservative circles viewed Hook as one of the gurus of the neoconservative revival during the 1970s and 1980s. In the 1960s Shachtmanism aligned with the Democratic Party and was also involved with the New Left. By the mid 1960s such was the Shachtmanite opposition to the USSR that they had arrived on issues of American foreign policy that were the same as Hook's, including supporting the American presence in Vietnam. In 1972 the Shachtmanists endorsed Leftist Senator Henry Jackson for the Democratic presidential nomination against Leftist George McGovern whom they regarded as an appeaser toward the USSR. Jackson was both pro-war and vehemently anti-Soviet, advocating a 'hawkish' position on foreign policy towards the USSR. Like Hook, Jackson was also awarded the Medal of Freedom by President Reagan in 1984.

At this time Tom Kahn, a prominent Shachtmanite and an organizer of the AFL-CIO, who will be considered below, was Senator Jackson's chief speechwriter.[72] Many of Jackson's aides were to become prominent in the oddly named 'neo-conservative' movement, including veteran Trotskyites Paul Wolfowitz, Elliott Abrams, Richard Perle, and Douglas Feith, and all of whom became prominent in the Administration of President George H

---

71   Again, there is obfuscation with the use of the term 'anti-Communist'. What is meant in such cases is not opposition to Communism, but opposition to Stalinism, and the course the USSR had set upon after the elimination of the Trotskyites, et al. Many of these so-called 'anti-Communists' in opposing the USSR considered themselves loyal to the legacy of Trotsky.

72   Tom Kahn, 'Max Shachtman: His Ideas and His Movement', Editor's Note on Kahn, *Dissent Magazine*, 252 http://www.dissentmagazine.org/democratiya/article_pdfs/d11Khan.pdf

W Bush, all of whom helped to instigate the present war against Islam, which they began to call 'Islamofascism', as a new means of extending American world supremacy.

Tom Kahn, who remained an avid follower of Shachtman, explained his mentor's position on the USA in Vietnam in this way, while insisting that Shachtman never compromised his Socialist ideals:

> His views on Vietnam were, and are, unpopular on the Left. He had no allusions about the South Vietnamese government, but neither was he confused about the totalitarian nature of the North Vietnamese regime. In the South there were manifest possibilities for a democratic development... He knew that those democratic possibilities would be crushed if Hanoi's military takeover of the South succeeded. He considered the frustration of the attempt to be a worthy objective of American policy...[73]

This position in its own right can be readily justified by dialectics, as the basis for the support of Trotskyist factions, including those of both Hook and Shachtman during the Cold War, and the present legacy of the so-called 'neo-cons' in backing American foreign policy as the manifestation of a 'global democratic revolution', as a development of Trotsky's 'world proletarian revolution.'

National Endowment for Democracy

It was from this milieu that the National Endowment for Democracy (NED) was formed, which took up from the CIA's Congress for Cultural Freedom.

President George W Bush embraced the world revolutionary mission of the USA, stating in 2003 to NED that the war in Iraq was the latest front in the 'global democratic revolution' led by the United States. 'The revolution under former president

---

73   Tom Kahn, Democratiya 11, 2007, reprinted in *Dissent Magazine*, *Ibid.*, 258.

Ronald Reagan freed the people of Soviet-dominated Europe, he declared, and is destined now to liberate the Middle East as well'.[74]

NED was established in 1983 at the prompting of Shachtmanist veteran Tom Kahn, and endorsed by an Act of US Congress introduced by Congressman George Agree. Carl Gershman,[75] a Shachtmanite, was appointed president of NED in 1984, and remains so. Gershman had been a founder and Executive Director (1974-1980) of Social Democrats USA (SD-USA).[76] Among the founding directors of NED was Albert Glotzer, a national committee member of the SD-USA, who had served as Trotsky's bodyguard and secretary in Turkey in 1931,[77] who had assisted Shachtman with founding the Workers Party of the United States.

Congressman Agree and Tom Kahn believed that the USA needed a means, apart from the CIA, of supporting subversive movements against the USSR. Kahn, who became International Affairs Director of the AFL-CIO, was particularly spurred by the need to support the Solidarity movement in Poland, and had been involved with AFL-CIO meetings with Leftists from Latin America and South Africa.[78]

---

74 Fred Barbash, 'Bush: Iraq Part of 'Global Democratic Revolution': Liberation of Middle East Portrayed as Continuation of Reagan's Policies', *Washington Post*, 6 November 6, 2003.

75 Gershman served as Senior Counsellor to the United States Representative to the United Nations beginning in 1981. As it happens, the Representative he was advising was fellow Social Democrats comrade, Jeane Kirkpatrick, who had begun her political career in the (Trotskyist) Young People's Socialist League, a branch of the Shachtmanist-orientated Socialist Party, as had many other 'neo-cons.'

76 The Social Democrats USA had originated in 1972 after a split with the Trotskyist-orientated Socialist Party. The honorary chairman of the Social Democrats USA until his death in 1984 was Prof. Sidney Hook.

77 Glotzer was a leading Trotskyist. Expelled from the Communist Party USA in 1928 along with Max Shachtman, they founded the Communist League and the subsequent factions. When the Socialist Party factionalised in 1972 Glotzer joined the Social Democrats – USA faction, which remained closest to Shachtmanism, and which supported US foreign policy. Even in 1981 Glotzer was still involved with luminaries of the Socialist Workers Party. "British Trotskyism in 1931", Encyclopaedia of Trotskyism Online: Revolutionary History, http://www.marxists.org/history/etol/revhist/backiss/vol1/no1/glotzer.html (Accessed 7 March 2010).

78 Rachelle Horowitz, "Tom Kahn and the Fight for Democracy: A Political Portrait and Personal Recollection", *Dissent Magazine*, pp. 238-239. http://www.dissentmagazine.

Kahn had joined the Young Socialist League, the youth wing of Shachtman's Independent Socialist League,[79] and the Young People's Socialist League, which he continued to support until his death in 1992. Kahn was impressed by the Shachtman opposition to the USSR as the primary obstacle to world socialism.[80] He built up an anti-Soviet network throughout the world in 'opposition to the accommodationist policies of détente'.[81] There was a particular focus on assisting Solidarity in Poland from 1980.[82] Racehlle Horowitz's eulogy to Kahn ends with her confidence that had he been alive, he would have been a vigorous supporter of the war in Iraq.[83]

NED is funded by US Congress and supports 'activists and scholars' with 1000 grants in over 90 countries.[84] NED describes its program thus:

> From time to time Congress has provided special appropriations to the Endowment to carry out specific democratic initiatives in countries of special interest, including Poland (through the trade union Solidarity), Chile, Nicaragua, Eastern Europe (to aid in the democratic transition following the demise of the Soviet bloc), South Africa, Burma, China, Tibet, North Korea and the Balkans. With the latter, NED supported a number of civic groups, including those that played a key role in Serbia's electoral breakthrough in the fall of 2000. More recently, following 9/11 and the NED Board's adoption of its third strategic document, special funding has been provided for countries with substantial Muslim populations in the Middle East, Africa, and Asia.[85]

---

org/democratiya/article_pdfs/d11Horowitz.pdf (Accessed 8 March 2010).

79   *Ibid.* 209.

80   *Ibid.* 211.

81   *Ibid.,* 234.

82   *Ibid.,* 235.

83   *Ibid.,* 246.

84   'About NED', National Endowment for Democracy, http://www.ned.org/about (accessed 7 March 2010).

85   David Lowe, 'Idea to Reality: NED at 25: Reauthorization', NED, http://www.ned.org/about/history (accessed 7 March 2010).

NED therefore serves as a kind of 'Comintern' of the so-called 'American democratic revolution' throughout the world. The subversion by the USA, culturally, politically, and economically, with its front-groups, spies, fellow-travellers, activists, and outright revolutionaries, is more far-reaching than the USSR's allegedly 'communist' subversion ever was.

The accusation by the Stalinists at the Moscow Trials of the 1930s was that the Trotskyists were agents of foreign powers and would reintroduce capitalism. The crisis in Marxism caused by the Stalinist regime – the so-called 'betrayal of the revolution' as Trotsky himself termed it - resulted in such outrage among the Trotskyites that they were willing to whore themselves and undertake anything to bring down the Soviet edifice.

V

The Origins of the Cold War:

How Stalin Foiled a 'New World Order'

A fact unrealised by most on both the Right and the Left is that if it was not for Stalin a World State would have been imposed immediately after World War II. The USSR by an irony of history, stood for nationalism against the internationalism of the USA. The USSR was a bastion of conservatism and tradition; while the USA remains a centre of world revolution, the 'colour revolutions' sponsored by the National Endowment for Democracy, and many other globalist fronts, being present-day evidence of a process that has been taking place since the internationalist administration of President Woodrow Wilson, his 'Fourteen Points' for re-organising the world, and his promotion of the abortive League of Nations, the precursor of the United Nations.

While sections of the American Right, such as the John Birch Society, warned that the United Nations (UN) was a 'communist plot' to rule the world, they were correct in their critique of the UN on many points except one of major importance: it was Stalin who stymied the American globalist plan to use the UN as the basis for a 'one world government', a concept that was condemned by the USSR in favour of nationalism.

Russia: The Perennial Disappointment (To the Globalists)

Russia has never fitted well into the plans of those seeking to impose a uniform system upon humanity. Russia has remained untamed in terms of the sophisticated Western liberals seeking to establish a unipolar global world. Conservative philosophers, especially in Germany, such as Oswald Spengler, despite their opposition to Communism, could see that Bolshevik Russia

123

would soon jettison Marxist dogma and transform into a nationalist state and empire.

Russia's economy was regarded as backward by Western financiers and many bankers and industrialists not only welcomed the March and the November 1917 Revolutions,[1] but also provided backing for the revolutionaries to overthrow the Czarist regime.[2]

Industrialists and financiers looked optimistically to a post-Czarist Russia with a new government that would embark on industrialization, which implied the need for foreign capital and expertise, regardless of the revolutionary rhetoric about foreign capitalists. However, Stalin, even at this embryonic stage of the Soviet regime, was the spoiler. While Trotsky wished to pursue foreign investment,[3] as had been the case under Lenin's New Economic Policy,[4] Stalin dealt some swift blows to the broadly termed opposition bloc led by Trotsky, and pursued a course that was not amicable to foreign capital.

---

1   Jacob H Schiff, 'Jacob H Schiff Rejoices, By Telegraph to the Editor of the New York Times', March 18, 1917. This can be viewed at *The New York Times* online archives: http://query.nytimes.com/mem/archive-free/pdf?res=9802E4DD163AE532A2575BC1A 9659C946696D6CF
Jacob Schiff, 'Loans easier for Russia', *The New York Times*, 20 March 1917. http://query.nytimes.com/mem/archive-free/pdf?res=9B04EFDD143AE433A25753C2A9659 C946696D6CF
John B Young (National City Bank) 'Is A People's Revolution', *The New York Times*, March 16 1917.
'Bankers here pleased with news of revolution', *Ibid.*
'Stocks strong – Wall Street interpretation of Russian News', *Ibid.*
2   'Bolsheviki Will Not Make Separate Peace: Only Those Who Made Up Privileged Classes Under Czar Would Do So, Says Col. W B Thompson, Just Back From Red Cross Mission', *The New York Times*, January 27 1918.
3   Armand Hammer of Occidental Petroleum, who had been a concessionaire at the earliest stages of the Soviet regime, stated of his meeting with Trotsky that he was questioned as to how US capitalists regarded Russia as a 'desirable field for investment?' Trotsky, having returned from the Urals, thought that the region had great possibilities for American capital. Armand Hammer, *Hammer: Witness to History* (London: Coronet Books, 1988), 160.
4   Lenin had stated to Hammer: 'The New Economic Policy demands a fresh development of our economic possibilities. We hope to accelerate the process by a system of industrial and commercial concessions to foreigners. It will give great opportunities to the United State'. *Ibid.*, 143.

With the outbreak of war between Germany and the USSR, there was renewed hope for Russia being integrated into a post war new world order. Stalin relied on Western technology for his war machine in fighting the Germans.[5] However Stalin was not about to become America's junior partner in a post-war 'new world order', despite all the friendly rhetoric that had been spoken during World War II.

United Nations – Basis for World Parliament

Things seemed very jovial between 'Uncle Joe',[6] Roosevelt, and Churchill while the common enemy was being fought. Having secured the appeasement of the Allies at Potsdam for the establishment of a new Russian Empire over Eastern Europe and the Baltic states, Stalin was not about to compromise Russia's position of strength.

The first break in the wartime alliance came with America's grand new design to establish the United Nations as a world parliament, just as President Woodrow Wilson had tried a similar scheme with the League of Nations after World War I. The American plan for the UN called for power to be vested with the UN General Assembly, based on a parliamentary-type majority vote of the member states, with the USA able to buy the votes with the bribes of foreign aid and loans, such as Marshall Aid. Under such a system the Soviet bloc would have been outvoted and subservient to US policy behind the façade of the 'international community'. The Soviet position, on the other hand, was to make the UN Security Council the final arbiter of decisions with member states having the right to veto. Andrei Gromyko, Soviet foreign minister, summed up the situation:

> The US position in fact allowed the UN to be turned into an instrument for imposing the will of one group of

---

5   Antony Sutton, *National Suicide: Military Aid to the Soviet Union* (New York: Arlington House, 1973).

6   For Roosevelt's commitment to friendship with Stalin see the CIA essay: Gary Kern, How "Uncle Joe" Bugged FDR, Central Intelligence Agency, https://www.cia. gov/library/center-for-the-study-of-intelligence/csi-publications/csi-studies/studies/ vol47no1/article02.html

states upon another, above all the Soviet Union as the sole socialist member of the Council.[7]

Despite long standing conservative conspiracy theories regarding the UN being a Soviet plot to create a communist controlled World State,[8] it was the USSR that rendered the UN redundant as a method of imposing a new world order, thanks to the Soviet insistence on national – or imperial – sovereignty for itself and its power bloc.

Baruch Plan to 'Internationalise' Atomic Energy

The second pillar for the creation of a post-war new world order rested on the supposed 'internationalisation' of the awesome power of atomic energy. Like the democratic façade of the American plan for a UN General Assembly world parliament, this 'internationalisation' was perceived by the USSR as really meaning US control.

Dr Carroll Quigley[9] described the post-war situation leading to the Cold War, stating that the immediate policy of the USA rested on free trade and aid via the Marshall Plan, which would have included assistance for economic recovery to the Soviet bloc. However Stalin saw this as a means for the USA to establish its pre-eminence in the post war era. Quigley, a liberal globalist who saw the 'hope' of the world being through a world government and the 'tragedy' being its rejection,[10] wrote:

> On the whole, if blame must be allotted, it may be placed at the door of Stalin's office in the Kremlin. American willingness to co-operate continued until 1947, as is evident from the fact that the Marshall Plan offer of American aid

7   *A A Gromyko, Memories.* (London: Arrow Books, 1989).

8   For example, G Edward Griffin, *The Fearful Master: A Second Look at the United Nations* (Boston: Western Islands, 1964).

9   Quigley was an eminent historian and governmental adviser, and taught at Foreign Services School, Georgetown University, Harvard and Princeton universities. President Clinton spoke of Quigley as his adviser when at Harvard.

10 Hence the title of Quigley's magnum opus, *Tragedy and Hope* (New York: MacmillanCo., 1966).

for a co-operative Europe recovery effort was opened to the Soviet Union, but it now seems clear that Stalin had decided to close the door on co-operation and adopted a unilateral policy of limited aggression about February or March of 1946. The beginning of the Cold War may be placed at the date of this inferred decision or may be placed at the later and more obvious date of the Soviet refusal to accept Marshall Aid in July 1947.[11]

Quigley refers to the American initiative for atomic energy 'internationalisation' and how Stalin again scotched this strategy for US world domination:

> The most critical example of the Soviet refusal to co-operate and of its insistence on relapsing into isolation, secrecy, and terrorism is to be found in its refusal to join in American efforts to harness the dangerous powers of nuclear fission.[12]

A US State Department committee under Undersecretary of State Dean Acheson and Dr David Lilienthal, in conjunction with a 'second committee of citizens', led by the international banker and perennial presidential adviser Bernard Baruch, were convened in 1946 to draft a plan for 'some system of international control of nuclear energy'. Baruch presented the plan to the UN General Assembly on June 14 1946.[13]

Under this plan, the UN would own, control, or licence all uranium from the mine through processing and use, with operation of its own nuclear facilities throughout the world, inspection of all other such facilities, absolute prohibition of all nuclear bombs or diversion of nuclear materials to non-peaceful purposes, and punishment for evasion or violation of its regulations free from the Great Power veto which operated in the UN Security Council.[14]

11   Caroll Quigley, *Tragedy and Hope, Ibid.,* 892.
12   *Ibid.,* 893.
13   *Ibid.,* 895.
14   *Ibid.*

This was therefore a method of trying to bypass the problem of veto that had been insisted upon by the USSR to ensure its sovereignty, which had from the start rendered the UN impotent as a world-governing authority. Quigley laments that this 'generous offer' by the USA, '...was brusquely rejected by Andrei Gromyko on behalf of the Soviet Union within five days...'[15] Quigley pointed out that one of the main points the USSR raised in rejecting the Baruch Plan[16] was that there must be no tampering with the Great Power veto at the UN Security Council. Gromyko recalling his time as Soviet representative on the UN Atomic Energy Commission, states of the Baruch Plan:

> The actual intention was to be camouflaged by the creation of an international body to monitor the use of nuclear energy. However, Washington did not even try to hide that it intended to take the leading part in this body, to keep in its own hands everything to do with the production and storage of fissionable material and, under the guise of the need for international inspection, to interfere in the internal affairs of the sovereign nations.[17]

Baruch told Gromyko that experts would inspect all industries dealing with fissionable material. Gromyko remarked: 'Inevitably at that time they would all be Americans'.

Quigley's moral indignation at the USSR's rejection notwithstanding, we are now in a position of hindsight, considering recent world events, to understand Soviet suspicions. The moral choice is not as clear-cut as Quigley supposed. Japan had been A-bombed whilst seeking peace terms, their only real condition being the sanctity of their Emperor. America's position was unconditional, and of course it can be assumed that the Administration knew the Japanese could not accede to anything that would compromise Hirohito or the imperial house. Allen Dulles, who became head of the CIA, related in

---

15   *Ibid.*
16   Bernard Baruch, The Baruch Plan, 1946. http://www.atomicarchive.com/Docs/
     Deterrence/BaruchPlan.shtml
17   A A Gromyko, op.cit.

an interview in 1963 that he had been in contact with Japanese factions that were in a position to sue for peace,[18] and that the sole Japanese concern was that the Emperor would be left alone. 'Just weeks later... Hiroshima and Nagasaki were bombed'.[19] The Americans in bombing Japan sought to impress upon Stalin the need to continue their wartime alliance into the post-war world, with the USSR as a junior partner at best. Veteran journalist Robert Fisk comments on the bombing of Japan:

> Stalin was finally impressed by the effect of Truman's new weapon at Hiroshima. He very much wanted the bomb for Russia. When US proposals to limit the bomb to America alone were uncompromising, Stalin's scientists accelerated their work.[20]

Even Britain was concerned at US intentions, Prime Minister Clement Atlee explaining:

> We had to hold up our position vis-à-vis the Americans. We couldn't allow ourselves to be wholly in their hands... We had worked from the start for international control of the bomb... We could not agree that only America should have atomic energy...[21]

Were both the USSR and Britain being selfish, as implied indignantly by Quigley? Bernard Baruch himself stated:

> The gains of our scientists, our engineers, our industrialists, produced the supreme weapon of all time — the atomic bomb. That we shall never give away, until and unless security for us, for the world, is established. Until that time comes, the US will remain the guardian of safety. We can be trusted....[22]

---

18 Dulles suspected that the peace initiative came from the Emperor himself.
19 'Ladies of the Press', panel-interview programme, WOR-TV, New York, January 19, 1963. http://www.greenwych.ca/dulles.htm
20 Bob Fisk, "The Decision to Bomb Hiroshima and Nagasaki," 11, 1983. The article can be found at: http://www.greenwych.ca/hiro2bmb.htm
21 *Ibid.*
22 Bernard Baruch, NY Tribune, April 17, 1947. cited by Fisk, *Ibid.*

The rhetoric by Baruch about the USA being the 'trusted guardian' of world peace and freedom is the same mantra the world has heard from President Woodrow Wilson to President Obama: Trust the US to act as the world's policeman.

Pacifist guru Bertrand Russell wrote in 1946 in the *Bulletin of Atomic Scientists*, expressing the type of hatred widely felt by globalists for the USSR after World War II, because of the Soviet rejection of a one world government. Russell, who was to play a key role along with many other eminent liberals and leftists as Stalin-hating Cold Warriors in the CIA founded Congress for Cultural Freedom,[23] makes it plain that the atomic bomb represented the ace card to the forcible establishment of a one world state:

> The American and British governments... should make it clear that genuine international co-operation is what they most desire. But although peace should be their goal, they should not let it appear that they are for peace at any price. At a certain stage, when their plans for an international government are ripe, they should offer them to the world... If Russia acquiesced willingly, all would be well. If not, it would be necessary to bring pressure to bear, even to the extent of risking war.[24]

Russell proposed what was clearly the intention of the US Administration and other globalists in assuring that atomic energy would be monopolised by an 'international agency' with power to act against any state reticent about being subjected to a one world state:

> It is entirely clear that there is only one way in which great wars can be permanently prevented, and that is the establishment of an international government with a monopoly of serious armed force. When I speak of an international government, I mean one that really governs,

23   Frances Stonor Saunders, op. cit., 91.
24   Bertrand Russell, 'The Atomic Bomb and the Prevention of War', *Bulletin of Atomic Scientists*, October 1, 1946, 5.

not an amiable façade like the League of Nations, or a pretentious sham like the United Nations under its present constitution. An international government, if it is to be able to preserve peace, must have the only atomic bombs, the only plant for producing them, the only air force, the only battleships, and, generally, whatever is necessary to make it irresistible. Its atomic staff, its air squadrons, the crews of its battleships, and its infantry regiments must each severally be composed of men of many different nations; there must be no possibility of the development of national feeling in any unit larger than a company. Every member of the international armed force should be carefully trained in loyalty to the international government.

The international authority must have a monopoly of uranium, and of whatever other raw material may hereafter be found suitable for the manufacture of atomic bombs. It must have a large army of inspectors who must have the right to enter any factory without notice; any attempt to interfere with them or to obstruct their work must be treated as a casus belli. They must be provided with aeroplanes enabling them to discover whether secret plants are being established in empty regions near either Pole or in the middle of large deserts.[25]

Note that Russell is already by this time disparaging of the UN as having been rendered useless as an 'international government' by the USSR. His proposals are akin to those of the USA's Baruch Plan. Russell made it clear where he stood in terms of American global hegemony:

In the near future, a world war, however terrible, would probably end in American victory without the destruction of civilisation in the Western hemisphere, and American victory would no doubt lead to a world government under the hegemony of the United States — a result which, for my part, I should welcome with enthusiasm.[26]

---

25   *Ibid.,* 2.
26   *Ibid.,* 3.

Contingent upon the usefulness of the UN as a global government was the elimination of the Soviet-imposed veto in the UN Security Council:

> If the United Nations Organisation is to serve any useful purpose, three successive reforms are necessary. First, the veto of the Great Powers must be abolished, and majorities must be declared competent to decide on all questions that come before the organisation; second, the contingents of the various Powers to the armed forces of the organisation must be increased until they become stronger than any national armed forces; third, the contingents, instead of remaining national blocks, must be distributed so that no considerable unit retains any national feeling or national cohesion. When all these things have been done, but not before, the United Nations Organisation may become a means of averting great wars.[27]

In 1961 Russell, in considering the Soviet attitude to the Baruch Plan and the UNO, stated that:

> it was Stalin's Russia, flushed with the pride in victory over the Germans, suspicious (not without reason) of the Western Powers, and aware that in the United Nations it could almost always be outvoted.[28]

CFR Blueprint for Cold War

When Stalin scuttled the UN as the basis for an 'international government' a re-evaluation of the USSR was made by America's self-described 'foreign policy establishment', the Council on Foreign Relations (CFR).[29]

CFR historian Peter Grosse states that the internationalist proposals for a post-war new world order were met with a firm

27　*Ibid.*

28　Bertrand Russell, *Has Man a Future?* (Hammondsworth: Penguin Books, 1961), 25.

29　Peter Grosse in his semi-official history of the CFR, calls the Council 'the East Coast foreign policy establishment'. P Grosse, *Continuing the Inquiry*, op. cit., Chapter: 'X' Leads the Way,'http://www.cfr.org/about/history/cfr/x_leads.html

'nyet' from the USSR: 'In characteristic fashion, [CFR] Council planners conceived a study group to analyze the coming world order'. What they envisaged was a joint CFR-Soviet study group to prepare proposals for what Grosse calls the 'coming world order' (sic):

> Percy Bidwell, director of the Council's new Studies Program, had courteously approached the Soviet Embassy as early as January 1944 to stimulate interest in the joint project. He was received by Ambassador Andrei Gromyko, whose response would become all too familiar in the years to come. Through Gromyko the Russian word 'nyet' entered the English language. Without any pretense of diplomatic tact, the ambassador (soon to be foreign minister) told the men from the Council he would not permit any responsible Soviet spokesman to join in such a discussion.[30]

Since Stalin rejected US post-war aims, a new policy towards the USSR was required. This policy was to be not one of direct military confrontation, but of 'containment', a word coined by American diplomat, veteran expert on Russia and CFR member George Kennan.[31] Grosse is candid in describing the 'behind-the-scenes' (sic) manner by which the CFR influenced Cold War policy:

> The Council on Foreign Relations functioned at the core of the public institution-building of the early Cold War, but only behind the scenes. As a forum providing intellectual stimulation and energy, it enabled well-placed members to convey cutting-edge thinking to the public—but without portraying the Council as the font from which the ideas rose.[32]

An initial report by George S Franklin in 1946 recommended attempting to work with the USSR as far as possible, 'unless and until it becomes entirely evident that the USSR is not interested

---

30   *Ibid.*, 'The First Transformation'.
31   *Ibid.*, 'X Leads the Way'. "X" was Kennan, an anonymous policy-maker.
32   *Ibid.*

in achieving cooperation…' However the USA should pursue co-operation from a position of military strength:

> The United States must be powerful not only politically and economically, but also militarily. We cannot afford to dissipate our military strength unless Russia is willing concurrently to decrease hers. On this we lay great emphasis.

> We must take every opportunity to work with the Soviets now, when their power is still far inferior to ours, and hope that we can establish our cooperation on a firmer basis for the not so distant future when they will have completed their reconstruction and greatly increased their strength…. The policy we advocate is one of firmness coupled with moderation and patience.[33]

However this mildly conciliatory policy was rejected. Grosse writes:

> The Franklin report of May 1946, outlining cautious hopes for cooperative relations between the United States and the Soviet Union in the coming post-World War II years, was dead. The board's committee on studies formally decided against publication in July; by November all sympathy for a conciliatory stance toward Moscow had disappeared from the corridors of the Harold Pratt House.[34]

The result was the era of the Cold War, where Trotskyites and other Marxists, liberal-internationalists, the CIA and American expansionists, and Zionists, all disappointed with the way the USSR had emerged since the rise of Stalin, jumped into bed on an anti-Soviet crusade.

---

33   *Ibid.*, "The First Transformation.,"http://www.cfr.org/about/history/cfr/first_transformation.html
34   *Ibid.*

Post-Cold War

The rise of Mikhail Gorbachev, who has since made a name for himself on the world stage as one of the globalist elite,[35] and the drunken interregnum of Boris Yeltsin, seemed as though Russia was at last about to come into the globalist fold. Whatever the influences that might have been working behind Soviet President Gorbachev when he dismantled the Soviet state, in 1991 he had created the Gorbachev Foundation for the purpose of planning Russia's 'place and role in the future world order', as well as having a broader policy of promoting 'globalization'.[36] Gorbachev also sees himself in a grander role, stating that, 'the keynote of the Foundation's activities is Toward a New Civilization'.[37]

The same year that Gorbachev created his Foundation to advocate a 'new world order' in tandem with other globalist think tanks such as the Soros Foundation and Open Society Institute, etc., President George H W Bush was enthusing that with the demise of the Soviet bloc a 'new world order' might at last emerge as envisaged by the founders of the UN:

> ...Until now the world we've known has been a world divided – a world of barbed wire and concrete block, conflict and cold war. Now we can see a new world coming into view. A world in which there is the very real prospect of a new world order... A world where the United Nations, freed from cold war stalemate, is poised to fulfil the historic mission of its founders...[38]

The globalists' hopes for Russia were yet again dashed with the advent of Vladimir Putin, and the emergence of influential forces even more antagonistic towards Russia's incorporation

---

35 K R Bolton, 'Mikhail Gorbachev: Globalist Super-Star', *Foreign Policy Journal*, April 3, 2011; http://www.foreignpolicyjournal.com/2011/04/03/mikhail-gorbachev-globalist-super-star/

36 The Gorbachev Foundation, "About Us, The Foundation Projects and Structural Subdivisions," http://www.gorby.ru/en/rubrs.asp?rubr_id=302

37 *Ibid.*

38 George H W Bush, speech before US Congress, March 6, 1991.

into a 'new world order'.[39] This includes a significant rise of Stalin nostalgia among Russians.

To the globalists Russia has – again – taken a 'wrong direction', the very title of a CFR policy paper. In Russia's Wrong Direction: What the United States Can and Should do, the hegemonic attitude of the US ruling clique is not even disguised. The report is replete with all the old Cold War rhetoric. It castigates Putin for placing Russia on a course in his domestic and foreign policies that 'cause problems for the United States'. The recommendation is for 'selective cooperation' rather than 'partnership, which is not now feasible'. The conclusion in the opening statement is that 'Russia is heading in the wrong direction'.[40]

Senators John Edward and Jack Kemp are acknowledged for their efforts in bringing 'international attention' to Putin's attempts to 'intimidate or put out of business foreign and Russian nongovernmental organizations'.[41] That is to say, Putin has resisted foreign-inspired organisations that derive from the international network of currency speculator George Soros and his Open Society Institute, National Endowment for Democracy, Freedom House, and a multitude of other so-called NGOs, that have been responsible for 'colour revolutions' and 'regime change' throughout the former Soviet bloc and further afield.[42]

The CFR Task Force Report laments that cooperation between Russia and the USA is now the exception rather than the norm. Russia is critiqued for 'becoming increasingly more authoritarian', while America's foreign policy is one of promoting 'democracy'

---

39   For example, the "Eurasian" concept whose chief proponent is Prof. Alexander Dugin, head of the Center for Conservative Research, Moscow State University, who advocates a "multi-polar" world of power bloc "vectors" as an alternative to globalization.

40   Jack Kemp, et al, Russia's Wrong Direction: What the United States Can and Should do, *Independent Task Force Report* no. 57 (New York: Council on Foreign Relations, 2006) xi. The entire publication can be downloaded at: http://www.cfr.org/publication/9997/

41   Richard N Haass, CFR President, *Ibid.*

42   K R Bolton, 'The Globalist Web of Subversion', *Foreign Policy Journal*, February 7, 2011; http://www.foreignpolicyjournal.com/2011/02/07/the-globalist-web-of-subversion/

throughout the word,[43] which is to say, overthrowing states that do not succumb to US hegemony with the use of the NGOs that Putin is condemned for 'intimidating'. Russia's policies on its 'periphery' are also of concern;[44] by which is meant that Russia does not desire hostile states on its borders, run by regimes that have been installed by those NGO's that Putin is 'intimidating' in Russia. The CFR therefore recommends that more should be done to 'accelerate the integration of those states into the West',[45] and thereby surround Russia with hostile states. The CFR recommends that US Congress interfere directly in the Russian political process by funding opposition movements in Russia under the façade of strengthening democracy, by increased funding for the Freedom Support Act, referring to the 2007-2008 presidential elections.[46] Of note is Mark F Brzezinski as one of the authors, who served on the National Security Council as an adviser on Russian and Eurasian affairs under Clinton, as his father Zbigniew served under Carter. Antonia W Bouis is cited as founding executive director of the Soros Foundations (1987-92); James A Harmon, senior advisor to the Rothschild Group, et al.

As has been alluded to previously, Putin is seen in US foreign policy and Russian oligarchic circles as continuing the legacy of Stalin.

---

43   *Ibid.*, 4.
44   *Ibid.*, 5.
45   *Ibid.*, 6.
46   *Ibid.*, 7.

VI

Who Killed Stalin?

Whether Stalin was murdered or died of 'natural causes' has long been a matter of debate. Certainly Stalin had made many enemies, but the character of these enemies is generally obscured by a focus on Stalin's alleged crimes. Hence relatively little is known of the titanic struggle Stalin waged against a myriad of anti-Russian forces, both within Russia and globally. Much of that struggle has been considered in the preceding chapters.

The Napoleon of Russia

Whatever crimes may be laid at Stalin's feet[1] there are several transcendent facts of history: (1) Stalin destroyed the virus of doctrinaire Bolshevism and reoriented Russia into a powerful state, rather than as a satrap of international finance, (2) Stalin thwarted the post-1945 plan of the globalists to establish a one world government under US hegemony. His arch-enemy, Trotsky, was correct in charging that Stalin has 'betrayed the Revolution' by repudiating much of the Marxist dogma[2] and in calling him a 'Bonapartist'.

Trotsky aptly made analogies between Russia and Jacobin France, and referred to 'Stalinist Bonapartism'.[3] Stalin had reversed Marxist doctrine in a manner similar to Napoleon's repudiation of Jacobin doctrines in France. Trotsky lamented, among much else, that the original Bolshevik policy of destroying the soul of Russia had been halted and was being

---

1   It is often overlooked that Stalin had inherited the totalitarian structure that had already been established by Lenin and Trotsky, who were hardly charitable in their dealings with opponents.
2   See Chapter 1.
3   Leon Trotsky, 'The Workers' State, Thermidor and Bonapartism', *International Socialist Review,* Vol.17 No.3, Summer 1956, 93-101, 105, http://www.marxists.org/archive/trotsky/1935/02/ws-therm-bon.htm

reversed: 'The storming of heaven, like the storming of the family, is now brought to a stop'.[4] Stalin repudiated these psychotic doctrines and established a strong national edifice that would create a European bloc[5] to withstand the onslaught of post-1945 American-imposed plutocratic hegemony.

We have already seen how Stalin purged Bolshevism of the 'rootless cosmopolitans' in both politics and the arts, repudiated 'world revolution' in favour of 'socialism in one country', and rejected US plans for a one world government via the United Nations. The purges of the late 1930s involved a disproportionate number of Jews who had been heavily represented in the Bolshevik apparatus, led by Trotsky, Zinoviev and Kamenev. Whatever suspicions World Jewry had towards Stalin were however temporarily allayed as the 'gallant Soviet army' fought the Nazis.

When Zionism was constructing its Israeli state in the British mandate of Palestine during and after World War II, the Zionists were supported both diplomatically and with weapons from the Soviet bloc.[6] Many of the founders of Israel therefore assumed that Stalin would remain a faithful ally, just as the USA assumed that their wartime alliance with the USSR would be maintained in the post-war world. However, Stalin realised that with the creation of Israel, the issue of 'dual loyalty' arose among Soviet bloc Jewry. Soon after the creation of the Israeli state in 1948 Stalin was in conflict with World Zionism, and the USSR remained a major obstacle to Zionist objectives after Stalin's death.

The Doctors' Plot

Stalin had originally supported the creation of Israel. This was a successful strategy to open the region up to Soviet penetration, rather than sympathy for Zionism. Indeed, Stalin has long been accused of 'anti-Semitism'.[7]

---

4   Leon Trotsky, The Revolution Betrayed, op. cit., http://www.marxists.org/archive/
     trotsky/1936/revbet/ch07.htm
5   Warsaw Pact and Comecom, military and economic blocs respectively.
6   K R Bolton, The Red Face of Israel, *Foreign Policy Journal*, 2 August 2010
     http://www.foreignpolicyjournal.com/2010/08/02/the-red-face-of-israel/all/1
7   Arkady Vaksberg, *Stalin Against the Jews* (New York: Alfred A Knopf, 1984), inter

In 1952, a year before Stalin's death, an epochal event occurred in Czechoslovakia, the trial and hanging of mainly Jewish leaders of the Communist Party, led by Party General Secretary Rudolf Slansky, who had been arrested in 1951. The following year Slansky and thirteen co-defendants were tried as 'Trotskyite-Titoist-Zionist traitors'. The defendants were accused of espionage and economic sabotage, and of working on behalf of Yugoslavia, Israel and the USA.

Many other Jews were mentioned as co-conspirators, and were implicated in a cabal that included influential US Supreme Court Justice Felix Frankfurter, described as a 'Jewish nationalist', and Mosha Pijade the 'Titoist Jewish ideologist 'in Yugoslavia. It was alleged that a conspiracy against the state had been hatched at a secret meeting in Washington in 1947, between President Truman, Secretary of State Acheson, former Treasury Secretary Henry Morgenthau Jr., and Israeli leaders David Ben Gurion and Moshe Sharett. In the indictment Slansky was described as 'by his very nature a Zionist' who had, in exchange for American support for Israel, agreed to place 'Zionists in important sectors of Government, economy, and Party apparatus'. The plan included the assassination of President Gottwald by a 'freemason' doctor.[8]

These factors were to emerge a year later in the USSR in the so-called 'Doctors' Plot'. This allegedly involved hundreds of doctors and was centred on the death in 1948 of A A Zhdanov, Stalin's likely successor, who had formulated the doctrine on Soviet arts[9] that repudiated 'rootless cosmopolitanism', which was often synonymous with 'Jewishness'. After several years of investigation, Stalin had intended to use this increasingly wide-ranging plot to undertake a comprehensive campaign against Jewish influence.

The 'case of the doctors' as it was officially called, linked the doctors with American intelligence and the Soviet Ministry of

---

alia.

8   Paul Lendvai, *Anti-Semitism in Eastern Europe* (London: Macdonald & Co., 1972), 243-245.
9   See Chapter II.

State Security (MGB).[10] Additionally, members of the Jewish Antifascist Committee were linked to the 'Doctors' Plot', and to spying for the USA,[11] tried in 1952 and executed, as part of the campaign against 'rootless cosmopolitism'.[12] On December 1, at a meeting of the Presidium of the Central Committee of the Communist Party, Stalin declared, 'every Jew is a potential spy for the United States'.[13]

The Soviet secret police had always had a disproportionate number of Jews, and was the power base of Lavrenti Beria. Brent and Naumov state that Stalin wished to remove Beria and that a file was said to have been compiled on him.[14] The rumour of a 'Day X' when Jews would be deported en masse to Siberia spread throughout the Jewish population.[15]

It is in these circumstances that Stalin died in March 1953.

Stalin's Death

The death of Stalin seems to have involved two rival factions for the leadership of Russia, one centred on Khrushchev and supported by the military, and the other centred on Beria and supported by the MGB. Given that Zhdanov, Stalin's likely successor, had died in 1948, prompting the accusations of murder, it does not seem too fanciful that he was indeed eliminated, and the likely culprit was Beria, who had been his rival since the war years. Beria in alliance with Malenkov initiated the 'Leningrad affair' in 1950; a purge of Zhdanov's associates. At this time Khrushchev began to be regarded as an alternative to a Beria-Malenkov regime after Stalin.

With Beria's control over security affairs, Stalin's bodyguard was changed shortly before his death. Alexandr Proskrebychev,

---

10   J Brent and V P Naumov, *Stalin's Last Crime: The Doctors' Plot* (London: John Murray, 2004), 1-10.
11   *Ibid.*, 214.
12   *Ibid.*, 94.
13   *Ibid.*, 184.
14   *Ibid.*, 258.
15   *Ibid.*, 297.

Stalin's personal secretary since 1928, was placed under house arrest. Lt-Colonel Nikolay Vlasik, Chief of Stalin's personal security for 25 years, was arrested on December 16, 1952 and died several weeks later in prison.[16] Major-General Petr Kosynkin, Vice-Commander of the Kremlin Guard, responsible for Stalin's security, and according to Peter Deriabin,[17] the only surviving member of the bodyguard whom Stalin trusted, died of a 'heart attack' on February 17 1953. Deriabin comments: '[This] process of stripping Stalin of all his personal security [was] a studied and very ably handled business'.[18]

The accounts of Stalin's death on March 5 1953 vary widely and are contradictory. Amy Knight writes that 'Members of the leadership may have deliberately delayed medical treatment for Stalin – probably for at least ten or twelve hours – when they knew he was seriously ill'.[19] The commonly stated time of Stalin's death is 9:50 PM, yet Dimitry Volkogonov, who has had access to the classified documents on the subject in the Russian archives, states that the actual time was 9: 50 AM.[20]

The ten doctors who attended Stalin during his illness did not complete their report until July 1953. It had gone through at least two drafts, which vary from each other 'in significant respects', marked 'top secret' and submitted to the Central Committee of the Communist Party. Brent and Naumov comment, 'The final draft is probably supervised by Beria'.[21]

What is known is that Stalin became ill following a dinner with Beria, Malenkov, Khrushchev and Bulganin that had begun the night of February 28 and ended in the early morning of Saturday, March 1. Khrushchev claimed that Stalin had been

---

16   Ludo Martens *Another view of Stalin* (1995 John Plaice, 1995), http://www.plp.org/books/Stalin/node153.html

17   Former counter-intelligence officer and member of Stalin's bodyguard who defected to the West in 1954.

18   P. Deriabin, *Watchdogs of Terror: Russian Bodyguards from the Tsars to the Commissars* (1984), 321;

19   Amy Knight, *Beria: Stalin's First Lieutenant* (Princeton, New Jersey: Princeton University Press, 1993), 179.

20   J Brent and V P Naumov, op. cit., 313.

21   *Ibid.,* 314.

'pretty drunk', but others stated that Stalin only drank fruit juice that night, and it is known that Stalin seldom drank hard liquor.[22] Khrushchev claimed that the evening went well, with Stalin in high spirits, while others claim that Stalin was angry that the 'Doctors' Plot' issue was not progressing. Stalin suddenly retired to his room and the party left, but they returned when hearing of Stalin's collapse. They stayed from March 2, until his death on March 5.

At Midday on March 1 there was no movement in Stalin's quarters. The servants and other personnel were prevented from entering, although the staff were becoming worried. At 6: 30 AM a light came on, indicating Stalin was working, which allayed the concerns of the staff. Some accounts state that Stalin was found at 10: 30 PM lying on the floor next to his desk. However, there are discrepancies in accounts as to when and how Stalin was found.[23] Khrushchev stated that he suggested delaying calling doctors, claiming that Stalin might have merely had a hangover, although it is now known that he had not been drinking. Beria likewise was not in a hurry to call for medical help.[24] Medical assistance was not permitted for at least ten hours after Stalin was found lying on the floor, although the standing order to the Kremlin Guard was that 'if any Kremlin official showed signs of illness, doctors were to be called immediately by the guards themselves', and there had been no requirement to seek the approval of Khrushchev, Beria or anyone else.[25] Brent and Naumov comment:

> Either the guards had been instructed to deviate from their standing order by members of the Politburo, or their call for help was countermanded. In either case, complicity at the highest level of Soviet government appears to have ensured that Stalin would die.[26]

According to V M Molotov, Minister of Foreign Affairs, Beria

---

22   *Ibid.*, 314-315. No high alcohol level was found in Stalin's blood or urine. 320.

23   *Ibid.*, 315.

24   *Ibid.*, 316.

25   *Ibid.*, 317.

26   *Ibid.*

boasted to him on May 1 1953 of Stalin's death: 'I did him in. I saved you all!'[27]

While the complicity of Khrushchev and Beria in Stalin's death seems undoubted, the question of a direct hand remains open. Was Stalin poisoned? Stalin suffered both a cerebral haemorrhage and stomach haemorrhaging. However references to stomach haemorrhaging were eliminated from the doctors' report to the Central Committee. Brent and Naumov question whether this was a cover-up to prevent suggestions of poisoning.[28] They raise the possibility that warfarin, a tasteless and colourless blood thinner also used as rat poison, might have been slipped by Beria into Stalin's drink. The right doses imbued over several days would cause cerebral and stomach haemorrhaging in someone already having acute hardening of the arteries, as Stalin did.[29]

All those associated with Stalin's care were quickly discharged, and most were sent out of Moscow.[30]

Aftermath

Immediately after Stalin's death, a meeting of the Presidium was held. Beria proposed Malenkov as President of the Council of Ministers, and Malenkov proposed Beria as Vice-President and Minister of Internal Affairs and State Security.

The first actions of the new regime included the arrest of N Proskrebychev, Stalin's secretary, who was sent to the small village of his birth and kept under MGB (Ministry for State Security) surveillance and house arrest.[31] M D Ryumin, who had led the inquiry into Zhdanov's death, was arrested and shot in 1954.

Brent and Naumov state that 'within a week' of Stalin's funeral a review of the 'Doctors' Plot' case was ordered, and all of the

27   *Molotov Remembers*, p. 237, cited by Brent and Naumov, *Ibid.*, 320.
28   J Brent and V P Naumov, *Ibid.*, 321.
29   *Ibid.*, 322.
30   *Ibid.*
31   *Ibid.*, 339.

accused were released and exonerated. All those involved with the Jewish Antifascism Committee were also exonerated.[32]

Beria aimed to re-orientate the direction the USSR, which would have led to its implosion decades before that was achieved by Gorbachev.[33] Thaddeus Wittlin states that from 1951 Beria was advocating a return to the free market along the lines of Lenin's New Economic Policy. He also opposed Stalin's Russification policy that sought to create a unified Soviet culture among the disparate peoples of the USSR.[34] Beria's foreign policy objectives were to move closer to the West and to restore relations with Tito's Yugoslavia.[35] He also sought to detach East Germany from the Soviet bloc and inaugurate a free market economy there. Stalin's suspicions of Beria were well justified.

Although Khrushchev became Party General Secretary, this was a position of lesser importance to that of Beria, who was the real power.

The Soviet bloc could clearly not survive Beria's regime, and one might well ask whether he was an agent of those interests – both within and outside the Soviet bloc - that Stalin had fought since 1928? Certainly his policies suggest this. The Army moved and disarmed the NKVD troops in Moscow under Beria's command. *Pravda* announced Beria's arrest on July 10 1953, for 'criminal activities against the Party and the State'. In December it was announced that Beria and six accomplices, 'in the pay of foreign intelligence agencies [had been] conspiring for many years to seize power in the Soviet Union and restore capitalism'. Beria was tried by a special tribunal[36] and he and his subordinates were executed on December 23 1953.

---

32   *Ibid.,* 325-327.

33   K R Bolton, 'Mikhail Gorbachev: Globalist Super-Star', *Foreign Policy Journal*, April 3 2011, http://www.foreignpolicyjournal.com/2011/04/03/mikhail-gorbachev-globalist-super-star/

34   Thaddeus Wittlin, *Commissar: The Life and Death of Lavrenti Pavlovich Beria* (New York: Macmillan, 1972), 354.

35   *Ibid.,* 363-365.

36   On the Crimes and Anti-Party, Anti-Government Activities of Beria, Plenum of the Central Committee of the Communist Party of the Soviet Union, July 2-7 1953.

Despite what appears to have been Khrushchev's role in Stalin's death, and his famous repudiation of Stalinism, under his leadership the Soviet bloc did not succumb by radically deviating from Stalin's path in the way Beria sought. The Soviet bloc remained the main obstacle to American-plutocratic hegemony until succumbing to pressures from within and without. While we today live under a de facto one-world government, if it had not been for Stalin's obstructionism we would likely have succumbed to a de jure one-world state over six decades previously.

VII

The USSR After Stalin's Death

Despite what appears to be Khrushchev's complicity in the death of Stalin, possibly because of little or no options in the face of Beria's power, Beria's succession to leadership was very short-lived. Khrushchev with his secret address to the Twentieth Congress of the Communist Party of the Soviet Union in 1956 seemed to be about to embark on a new course and he is generally credited with the 'de-Stalinization' of the Soviet bloc. Yet, until the assumption of Mikhail Gorbachev, the Soviet bloc, especially spanning the regimes from Khrushchev to Brezhnev, remained as nationalistically intransigent toward US globalism and cultural decay as it was under Stalin. Also notable was the Soviet bloc's continued opposition to Israel and to World Zionism.

Origins of Soviet Anti-Zionism

There had always been a conflict between Zionist Jews and secularist Jews in the socialist movements throughout the world. Secularist or 'apostate' Jews believed that the best means of combating 'anti-Semitism' was for Jews to abandon their separate ethnic identity and assimilate into a new world socialist society. Zionists to the contrary regarded assimilation as ethnic suicide and held that anti-Semitism could never be eliminated from Gentile societies. Their best course was therefore to separate. Into this mix there was an influential element that combined Zionism and socialism. Moses Hess, who had an early influence on Karl Marx, was a leading proponent of both Zionism and Socialism.[1]

---

1   Shlomo Avineri, *Moses Hess: Prophet of Communism and Zionis*m (New York University, 1985).

However, Karl Marx was a secularist Jew who was antagonistic towards what he considered to be the 'Jewish spirit' in capitalism. Given his own money-grubbing mentality, this might have been no more than psychological projection. Nonetheless, he believed that Jews needed 'emancipating' from their preoccupation with money, writing:

> Money is the jealous god of Israel, in face of which no other god may exist. ... The god of the Jews has become secularized and has become the god of the world. The bill of exchange is the real god of the Jew. His god is only an illusory bill of exchange. The chimerical nationality of the Jew is the nationality of the merchant, of the man of money in general. What is the secular basis of Judaism? Practical need, self-interest. What is the worldly religion of the Jew? Huckstering. What is his worldly God? Money. Very well then! Emancipation from huckstering and money, consequently from practical, real Judaism, would be the self-emancipation of our time.[2]

Antagonism towards the Jews was of long duration in Russia[3] and was the primary reason why so many Jews entered the revolutionary movements to overthrow the Czar. Russian anti-Semitism manifested organisationally in The Black Hundred who opposed capitalism as much as socialism, and perceived them as equally Jewish.[4]

Stalin, in his fight for leadership, was up against a large number of veteran Jewish Bolsheviks, Trotsky being the principal enemy, as we have seen. Although originally supporting the creation of the State of Israel in 1948, this was primarily a means by which the USSR could destabilise the Middle East and head-off Anglo-American and other rival influences in the region. It was a matter of realpolitik, of which Stalin was a master, not sympathy towards Zionism. The question of

---

2   Karl Marx, On the Jewish Question, 1844. www.marxists.org/archive/marx/
      works/1844/jewish-question/
3   Walter Laqueur, *The Black Hundred: The Rise of the Extreme Right in Russia*, (New
      York: Harper Perennial, 1993).
4   *Ibid.*

the loyalty of Jews in the USSR and wider Soviet bloc after World War II became a further factor in Stalin's antagonism towards Jewish interests, as their loyalties were divided with the establishment of Israel. Hence, in Stalinism the old Czarist suspicion of Jews was revived as a State policy with a justification that Marx himself had condemned the 'Jewish spirit' of capitalism and that there had been a conflict of interests, even among Jews themselves, between Zionism, Socialism and Socialist-Zionism going back to before the 1917 Bolshevik Revolution.

Winston S Churchill referred to this in 1920 in the aftermath of the Bolshevik Revolution, as a 'struggle for the soul of the Jewish people'.[5] In writing of Chaim Weizmann, who became first President to Israel, Laurence Krane states of this:

...Some Jews felt that the savior of the Jews would come through political reform such as communism or socialism. Others argued that assimilation would answer the problem of anti-Semitism and ease the economic hardships of the Jew. Still others maintained that immigration to Palestine, as Israel was called then, and by building up settlements in the Land would save the Jews from economic privation and exploitation.[6]

As in Czarist Russia, in the Soviet bloc from the time of Stalin, Jews via Zionism were again seen as subversives aligned with Israel and the capitalist powers. The USSR henceforth became a centre of resistance to Zionism, which was described with Marxist rhetoric as an agent of imperialism. Much effort was expended in exposing the character of Zionism not simply as the doctrine of the Israeli State, but as having worldwide ramifications.

---

5   Winston Churchill, 'Zionism versus Bolshevism: a struggle for the soul of the Jewish people', London: *Illustrated Sunday Herald*, February 8, 1920, 5.

6   Laurence Krane , 'Chaim Weizmann, Builder of Israel', *The Jewish Magazine,* October 2002, http://74.125.155.132/search?q=cache:iZ0Sh9qb5vkJ:www.jewishmag. com/60mag/weizmann/weizmann.htm

One representative example is entitled *Zionism: Instrument of Imperialist Reaction*, published in 1970.[7] The book is a collection of letters of protest against Zionism and Israel written to the Soviet press, mainly by Soviet Jews, and a selection of articles by various writers that had been published in the Soviet press. For example, Prof. Braginsky's article '*The Class Essence of Zionism*', originally published in *Pravda*,[8] drew on Marxist and Leninist thinking in regard to Jewish autonomy, stating that Jewish assimilation is the 'historically progressive process', alluding to Marx's position on the issue, and quoting Lenin.[9]

The 1952 Prague Trials of Slansky et al, accused of working for Israel, World Zionism and the USA against the State, and other moves against Zionism, were not lost on the radical Right in Europe and the USA. A faction of the Right saw the Soviet bloc as preferable to American global hegemony, and the USA as the harbinger of cultural decay. In the latter respect especially, they were very much in accord with the official Soviet attitude towards 'rootless cosmopolitanism'. Many German war veterans who had fought the USSR had no intention of doing so again for US interests, and Major-General Otto E Remer's Socialist Reich Party was a particular concern for the post-war Occupation Authorities for its advocacy of a 'neutralist' line during the Cold War. In the USA the bi-weekly anti-communist newspaper, *Common Sense*, adopted a vigorously pro-Soviet line, their primary columnist, Fred Farrel, a widely experienced and travelled veteran reporter, stated the newspaper's consistent line for several decades until its demise in the 1970s that, 'the best anti-Communists I have ever known were the Stalinists. They fought Communism with a cold deadly, remorseless, realistic efficiency'.[10]

The Prague scenario was repeated in 1968 in Czechoslovakia and in Poland. Paul Landvai writes of the 'Zionist plot' against Poland

---

7 I Braginsky, et al., *Zionism: Instrument of Imperialist Reaction*, (Moscow: Novosti Press Agency Publishing House, 1970).
8 I Bragnaski, *Ibid.*, '*The Class Essence of Zionism*'.
9 I Braginksy,*Ibid.,* 84.
10 F Farrel, 'The American Jewish Plot Against Europe', *Common Sense*, issue no. 598, 1 February, 1974, 2.

where the State accused Zionists of 'an open attack on the political system and its leaders' in the form of intellectual dissent and student demonstrations, which had been prompted by the State suppression of a student theatrical production. This State action was undertaken in the name of anti-Zionism, and factory and political meetings organised by the Communist party were held under the slogan 'Purge the Party of Zionists'.[11] Landvai states that since 1966, there had been a 'Jewish department' in the Ministry of Interior, led by Colonel Walichnowski, 'author of the anti-Zionist best-seller, *Israel and the Federal Republic of Germany*'.[12]

The 1967 Israeli Six Day War had instigated a new Soviet anti-Zionist campaign. In reaction dissident elements had begun to criticise the anti-Israel policy of the regime. The Czechoslovak Writers' Congress of 26-29 June 1967, addressed itself to the Party leadership. The Congress' pro-Israel position was aligned with demands for liberalisation.[13] During the May Day demonstration of 1967 students carried Israeli flags and placards demanding '*Let Israel Live*'. The philosophical faculty at Prague's Charles University issued a petition demanding the resumption of diplomatic relations with Israel.[14] The opening shots fired by Stalin at World Zionism only intensified after his death.

In 1969, just a year after the attempted weakening of the Soviet bloc through Czechoslovakia, The Publishing House for Political Literature in the USSR, published a particularly cogent book entitled *Caution, Zionism!* by Yuri Ivanov,[15] the chief Soviet expert on Israel. It is was wide-ranging book not only on Zionism

---

11   *Ibid.*, 113, 125.
12   *Ibid.*, 126.
13   *Ibid.* 263.
14   *Ibid.* 267.
15   Yuri Ivanov, *Caution, Zionism! Essays on the Ideology, Organisation and Practice of Zionism*, (Moscow: Progressive Publishers, 1970).
     The description on the back cover stated: 'Caution, Zionism! by Soviet Marxist historian Yuri Ivanov is a convincing exposé of modern Zionism as an ideology, a system of organisations and the practical policies of the wealthy Jewish bourgeoisie. Basing his arguments on numerous documents and facts, the author shows that Zionism has been and is a bellicose reactionary force working against the genuine national interests of all people, the Israeli people inclusive'. The book is online at: http://home.alphalink.com.au/~radnat/zionism/index.html

but also on Jewish history since ancient times, and is therefore something far more than simply 'anti-Zionist'. At the time of its distribution it caused Zionist objections throughout the world.

Pionerskaya *Pravda*, the newspaper of the 10,000,000 member Young Pioneers, carried an article in 1981 that stated, 'the major portion of American newspapers and television and radio companies are in Zionist hands'. The article stated, 'Jewish bankers and billionaires' were behind the Jewish Defense League, 'which terrorizes Soviet diplomats and other Soviet officials in the United States'. Pionerskaya claimed that 'most of the biggest monopolies for the production of weapons are controlled by Jewish bankers. Business and blood bring them enormous profits'[16]. The themes were very similar to those expressed by Ivanov in the widely distributed *Caution, Zionism!* There were many other such publications on Zionism published by the Soviet bloc and translated into various languages. These included: *In the Name of the Father and the Son* where the author states that 'American imperialism'[17] serves Zionism rather than the usual Soviet contention that Zionism serves American imperialism. *Creeping Counter-Revolution*, which states that 'anti-Semitism is an elemental response of the enslaved strata of the working populace to their barbaric exploitation by the Jewish bourgeoisie'.[18] *Invasion Without Arms*, stating that the 'chief strategic aim of Zion' is to maintain Jews as the 'ruling caste of capitalist society'. In words reminiscent of Stalin's campaign against 'rootless cosmopolitism', the author states that Zionists attempt to destroy 'national cultures' by promoting 'alien' and 'cosmopolitan ideas'.[19] In *Class Essence of Zionism* it is alleged that the creation of Israel gave rise to 'dual loyalty' among Jews towards the states in which they lived, and that they act as a subversive 'fifth column'. Zionist bankers and industrialists control the world through economic and political subterfuge, with the exception of the Soviet bloc, against which the Zionists were marshalling. [20]

---

16 *Pionerskaya Pravda*, 10 October 1981.
17 Ivan Shevtsov, *In the Name of the Father and the Son* (Moskovskii Rabochii, 1970).
18 V Begun, Creeping Counter-Revolution (Minsk, 1975).
19 V Begun, *Invasion Without Arms* (Minsk, 1977).
20 Lev A Korneyev, *Class Essence of Zionism* (Moscow, 1983).

Conclusion

With the demise of the USSR anti-Zionist ideologues, academics, activists and bureaucrats of the old Soviet regime entered the new regime, and continue the anti-Zionist legacy. Walter Laqueur has written of this 'anti-Semitism' in Russia from Czarist times, through the Soviet era to the present.[1] However, whether one calls it 'anti-Semitism' or a conflict between political systems, a Cold War II has emerged with the rise of Putin, whom many see as continuing in the style of Stalin, not least because of his intransigence, again reminiscent of Stalin, towards American designs for what is blatantly called a 'new world order'.

Many Nationalists, from Europe to the USA, as in Stalin's time, again see Russia as the most likely bulwark against American globalism and cultural decadence. For example, an organisation named Euro-Rus, a think tank of Right-wing academics promoting friendship with Russia as the basis for a united Europe, states that its aim is the creation of a 'European axis' based around 'Paris-Berlin-Moscow'. Delegates at the 2008 conference held in Belgium, the theme being 'Russia and the Building of European Thought', came from Russia, Belgium, Bulgaria, France, Netherlands, and Greece, and the USA.[2] Dr Pavel Tulaev, a seminal figure in the 'Russian New Right', also works for a Euro-Russian bloc that is not entangled with either the USA or China.

Should the Cold War, which only really had a thaw during the Gorbachev and Yeltsin interregnum, reach and even surpass

---

1   Walter Laqueur, op.cit.
2   Kris Roman, 'Euro-Rus: International Conference on Friday 27 and Saturday 28 June
     . Russia and the European Building Thought', June 6, 2008, http.//eurorusactivities.
     wordpress.com/2008/06/06/euro-rus-international-conference-on-friday-27-
     and-saturday-28-june-%E2%80%9Crussia-and-the-european-empire-building-
     thought%E2%80%9D/

the intensity of that of the 1950s and 1960s, as Russia seeks to reassert its position as a world power, the American radical Right, and indeed factions of the radical Right around the world, can be expected to intensify this pro-Russian outlook as they continue to see the potential of a revived Russia as a bulwark against a regime that is seen as more 'Semitic' than 'American'.

About the Author

Dr Kerry R Bolton has doctorates in theology and related areas, Ph.D. honoris causa and certifications in psychology and social work studies. He is a Fellow of the Academy of Social and Political Research (Athens), and a Member of T3 Indian Defence Research, a 'contributing writer' for Foreign Policy Journal, and a regular columnist for The Great Indian Dream (Indian Institute of Planning and Management) and New Dawn (Australia). He has been widely published by the scholarly and broader media.

Other Books by Kerry Bolton include:

Revolution from Above
(London: Arktos Media Ltd., 2011)

The Psychotic Left
(London: Black House Publishing, 2013)

Babel Inc.,
(London: Black House Publishing, 2013)

Artists of the Right
(San Francisco: Counter-Current Publishing, 2012)

Stalin: The Enduring Legacy
(Black House Publishing 2012)

Peron and Peronism
(Black House Publishing 2014)

Lightning Source UK Ltd.
Milton Keynes UK
UKHW051525191222
414059UK00014B/221